Reading for Justice

Reading for Justice

Engaging Middle Level Readers in Social Action through Young Adult Literature

Ashley S. Boyd and Janine J. Darragh

ROWMAN & LITTLEFIELD
Lanham • Boulder • New York • London

Published by Rowman & Littlefield
An imprint of The Rowman & Littlefield Publishing Group, Inc.
4501 Forbes Boulevard, Suite 200, Lanham, Maryland 20706
www.rowman.com

86-90 Paul Street, London EC2A 4NE

Copyright © 2023 by Ashley S. Boyd and Janine J. Darragh

All rights reserved. No part of this book may be reproduced in any form or by any electronic or mechanical means, including information storage and retrieval systems, without written permission from the publisher, except by a reviewer who may quote passages in a review.

British Library Cataloguing in Publication Information Available

Library of Congress Cataloging-in-Publication Data on File

ISBN 978-1-4758-6633-9 (cloth)
ISBN 978-1-4758-6634-6 (pbk.)
ISBN 978-1-4758-6635-3 (electronic)

For all the teachers—past, present, and future—who inspire youth to work toward a more just world.

Contents

Foreword	ix
Preface	xiii
Introduction	xv
Chapter 1: Coping With Trauma	1
Chapter 2: Social Class Disparities in the United States	13
Chapter 3: Bullying	25
Chapter 4: Refugee Crisis	39
Chapter 5: Indigenous Rights	51
Chapter 6: Sexual Orientation And Stigma	63
Chapter 7: Access And Disabilities	77
Chapter 8: Black Lives Matter	89
Chapter 9: Foster Care And Stigma	101
Chapter 10: Experiences of Immigrants	111
Conclusion	125
Index	127
About the Authors	129

Foreword

As we enter the twenty-third year of the twenty-first century, we are seeing an increasing sense of unrest around the ways we teach our young people. In particular, young adult literature is under attack by groups like Moms for Liberty. The irony is not missed. When examining Martin's (2022) list of *The Fifty Most Banned Books in America*, many of those books deal with issues of systemic oppression, most often around race and sexuality. Although there is a small, but vocal subset of people who feel as though the mere discussion of these topics will bring about the demise of our society, the reality is many of the students sitting in our classrooms are in fact navigating their own versions of many of the issues we are trying to shelter them from. As such, educators have a responsibility to support those students through their curricular choices. Additionally, it is critical that we begin to intentionally work on developing empathy in our young students in order to stitch our society back together in meaningful ways that benefit us all.

Young adult literature is one way to support our students in navigating their incredibly complex lives. As Rudine Sims Bishop (1990) proposed, books have the potential to be mirrors, windows and doors for students, and when we center novels with adolescents as the primary characters, they are more likely to find themselves. Additionally, they may be able to begin to find their peers through the books, and ultimately begin to remove the sense of "othering" that often occurs within our classrooms. If we are to have any hope of improving the way society relates to one another moving forward, it is critical that our young people find ways to see one another as human beings, particularly those people who are marginalized in one way or another. One aspect of this is by developing a sense of empathy.

Narrative has the potential to develop empathy (Alsup, 2015; Hays, 2021; Keen, 2006); although narrative alone may not move our students to positive and prosocial behavior (Falter, 2022). As Falter argues, there needs to be more done beyond reading to fully move students beyond a removed sense of empathy but instead towards real change. The key practices Falter (2022) presents include responsible listening, testimonial reading, critical witnessing, transmediation through embodied literacy, and action (p. 24).

Boyd and Darragh's book walks you through each of these ideas in various ways, creating spaces that fill the emotional void so often lost in the pursuit of common-core skills.

Reading for Justice: Engaging Middle Level Readers in Social Action Through Young Adult Literature is a powerful text that all middle-level teachers who want to prioritize student voice and civic engagement in their classrooms should have on their shelf. This book is easy to read and provides a simultaneously broad and in-depth examination of novels that might effect real change. One of the significant strengths of this book is the way the authors showcase the complexity of these issues and provide possible approaches and questions to help teachers lead their students through their emotional growth with these topics.

Boyd and Darragh's book explores multiple issues that are endemic to our society, including trauma, social class, bullying, the refugee crisis, Indigenous rights, sexual orientation and stigma, access and disabilities, Black Lives Matter, foster care, and immigrants. Each chapter follows a similar framework allowing for easy reference when planning, with the ability to selectively choose activities and texts, depending upon your focus. The chapters connect the proposed issue with a specific young adult text accompanied by multiple teaching strategies. An added bonus is that each chapter also presents optional texts that might be utilized for the same topic, allowing for more choice by the teacher. For example, the chapter on immigrants first begins by giving a brief overview of the state of immigration as it currently stands. Then it presents a brief introduction to the novel *Front Desk*, by Kelly Yang. Following a quick description, they delve into before-reading, during-reading, and after-reading teaching ideas that center many of the critical empathy approaches mentioned above, including responsible listening, testimonial reading, and critical witnessing. Following these explicitly guided teaching ideas, they move into the intersections that may exist with that particular novel. *Front Desk*, for example, may also be used to discuss racism, colorism, social classism, bullyism, refugeeism, and capitalism. Each of these is cross-referenced to other chapters to provide the educator with approaches to these heavy concepts. Many of the strategies mentioned within this section begin to move students towards the transmediation of literature, to further embody empathy for the readers around these issues.

Finally, each chapter ends with a section on taking social action. There are a variety of activities provided within each chapter that can be pulled across topics if desired. In the immigration chapter, for example, there are activities such as surveys for your math-minded students, campaigning to debunk stereotypes for more activist-minded students, and visual presentations for those students who thrive in visual literacies. This variety allows for a full exploration of the Universal Design of Learning (UDL) principles (CAST, 2018).

As Boyd and Darragh emphasize, "It is important, however, for teachers to not just focus on the struggles Mia and her family face, and to facilitate students also seeing the moments of joy and beauty in Mia's narrative" (Chapter 10). It is this very approach that lifts this book into the realm of critical empathy and prosocial behavior. It is imperative that we do not teach our students that having empathy and taking action are always done from a place of superiority, and this means that all students must recognize that there is joy in humanity, regardless of other issues one may face. This must not become a case of white saviorism.

I want to end my thinking by pulling from the authors' words themselves. "Although not the only place where social change is possible, education is one area where it can be made, and as such, we hope that teachers will embrace the opportunity—and responsibility—to create a better and more just world" (Conclusion).

—**Alice Hays, California State University, Bakersfield**

REFERENCES

Alsup, J. (2015). *Case for teaching literature in the secondary school*. Taylor and Francis.

Bishop, R. S. (1990). "Windows and mirrors: Children's books and parallel cultures." *Illinois English Bulletin, 78*(1), 83.

CAST. (2018). *Universal design for learning guidelines version 2.2*.

Falter, M. (2022). "When the shoes don't fit: A critical empathy framework for (young adult) literature instruction." *The ALAN Review*, 18–31.

Hays, A. (2021). *Engaging empathy and activating agency* (1st ed.). Rowman & Littlefield.

Keen, S. (2006). "A theory of narrative empathy." *Narrative, 14*(3), 207–236.

Martin, J. (2022, November 10). *The fifty most banned books in America*. CBS News.

Preface

In 2019, we published *Reading for Action: Engaging Youth in Social Justice through Young Adult Literature.* The response to this book by those for whom we wrote it—secondary teachers, librarians, school counselors, and teacher educators—was thrilling. When practicing teachers shared with us how they used it to implement curriculum and projects for social action in their classroom, we were humbled and ecstatic. Accompanying the responses from those who work with high school students, however, we began to receive requests for a similarly situated middle-school-level text. Teachers shared with us that they wanted to incorporate social action projects with their students, but they needed books, topics, and resource suggestions that related more fully to their younger, middle-level audiences. This book is a response to those calls.

We are both former secondary English Language Arts teachers and now teacher educators at public universities. We are passionate about our work to help our students become socially aware, culturally responsive, and critical teachers who cultivate those same dispositions in their own future students. As such, we believe that the world and its issues—the good, the bad, and the unmentionable—belong in our classrooms. If we do not teach students how to engage in discourse, weigh opinions, create informed knowledge, and take a stand, we are failing them. Furthermore, many of our students, including those in the middle grades, have firsthand experience with the types of social issues we describe in this text. They deserve to have their perspectives validated and the space to share stories like their own. We believe humans are never too young to make a positive change in their communities and world. We hope that the chapters that follow provide a window into accomplishing this work.

Introduction

In today's political climate, it is more imperative than ever that teachers work with students to understand, unpack, and address social issues. Society has become increasingly polarized on topics such as police brutality, immigration reform, and health care, and the media presents varied angles on these themes. Students must be equipped to read critically and respond intellectually to their ever-changing worlds. As evidenced by young people protesting for Black Lives Matter, speaking up about climate change, and advocating for mask mandates in schools, youth are ready to speak up and act. Often, however, they need the avenues and support for doing so. In this book, we posit young adult literature as one medium through which middle school teachers of English Language Arts can welcome social issues into their classrooms and facilitate youth civic action.

Young adult literature has been touted to enhance students' empathy, reflect their positionalities, and serve as a window to new cultures and worlds (Sims Bishop, 1990; Rezvi, Han, & Larnell, 2020; Sciurba, 2014). As such, texts (combined with effective teaching methods) can engage students with areas of social justice such as combating racism (Glenn, 2012), discerning the gender spectrum (Boyd & Bereiter, 2017), and promoting discussion of homophobia and heteronormativity (Blackburn & Clark, 2011). And while researchers have demonstrated that middle-level youth have a capacity for social justice, few have combined YAL and social justice to show *how* teachers can draw on books as springboards for civic action. For example, Miller (2014) invited her students to compose narrative essays about "perceived injustices they encountered" (p. 38) and promoted their "activist literacies" (p. 42). Coffey and Fulton (2018) similarly described projects in which middle school students participated in a critical service learning unit in which "students identified issues within their communities that were of concern to them" (p. 20), researched those topics, and created and implemented action plans. Stachowiak (2017) provided a framework for developing students' critical consciousness and leading them through social action projects, noting that in the end, middle-schoolers "changed policies for inclusivity [and] staged protests against discrimination" (p. 31). Thus while middle-grades youth are capable of critically thinking about their worlds and acting accordingly, tangible examples describing how such work can be accomplished is lacking in resources for teachers. This book provides a plethora of ideas for teachers on ways to cultivate youth's critical consciousness and embolden them to foster change.

This book illustrates, through specific textual examples and teaching strategies, how literature written for young adult audiences reflects current social topics and how educators can build on those works to incite middle-grades students to civic action. While our previous book (Boyd & Darragh, 2019a) focused on contemporary issues for high school youth, this project is in response to numerous requests from middle-grades educators for more resources for them. It therefore melds the fields of young adult literature, social action, and middle-level education with close attention to the practical aspects of teaching combined with theoretical perspectives on cultural issues.

OVERVIEW OF BOOK

We focus on ten contemporary social issues identified by professional educational organizations (e.g., NCTE, CEE, NEA) and teens as currently pressing: police brutality, social class disparities in the United States, sexual orientation and stigma, immigration reform, the refugee crisis, coping with trauma, Indigenous rights, foster care, access/disabilities, and bullying. We devote one chapter to each of these social topics alongside a specific novel written for middle-level readers and provide before-, during-, and after-reading strategies as well as ideas for students' social-action projects extending the focal topic. We also recommend companions surrounding the focal theme such as additional young adult literature, short stories, and poems, as well as related media for classroom use, including news sources and popular songs where applicable.

We know that the issues we cover are complex and that one of the strengths of young adult literature is its ability to portray overlapping categories of oppression and intersections in ways that authentically capture their complicated nature (Durand & Jiménez-García, 2018). Because of this, we include the section on intersections in each chapter and draw connections to illustrate for students how systems create and uphold inequity. We conceptualize chapters specifically as oft-perceived controversial social issues, rather than merely loosely as topics such as *gender* to ensure that they reflect identifiable matters that can be—and need to be—addressed and to make explicit the actual concrete *problem* at hand.

Language Matters

In addition, readers will see that almost every chapter begins its "before-reading" strategies with definitions and concepts. Our focus on language is intentional; we believe that discourse can both construct and reflect oppression (Fairclough, 1995) and therefore it is imperative that we ensure we are aware of our language practices. For example, the gender binary (men/women, boys/girls) is used so frequently in our everyday lives that many hardly notice it. However, such wording excludes individuals who do not identify within these two and is therefore wholly limiting. At the same time, then, we know that language has the power to disrupt and to dismantle structures of inequities when it is used to draw attention to issues or advocate for a cause. Instead of saying, "boys and girls" in a class, a teacher can simply say "class," "people," "scholars," or "humans." This small change is more inclusive and subverts the heteronormativity behind the binary. Furthermore, familiarizing students with the terminology related to each topic (e.g., refugees versus immigrants) makes them more informed about topics and able to participate in public discussions with confidence.

Social Action Projects

Finally, and related to this notion of public participation, each chapter includes a plethora of ideas for student social action projects. We firmly believe, however, that the ideas for these projects *should come from the students* (Boyd & Darragh, 2019a), and this point cannot be overstated. Our inclusion of the projects in this book is to provide suggestions and perhaps be used as a springboard for teachers and students to design their own. We have implemented social action projects at the middle and high school levels (Boyd & Miller, 2020) and at the university (Boyd & Darragh, 2019) and have found them highly engaging and rewarding for students. We use the *COAR* model (Boyd, 2017; Boyd & Darragh, 2019a; Boyd & Darragh, 2019b) in which students advance through a series of steps. They first select a social problem they want to address, narrowing it down from a broader concept. This point is crucial; if students stay at too broad of a level (e.g., mental health) instead of narrowing to an explicit problem (e.g., knowledge of mental-health resources at our school), they may be left feeling like there is not much they can do to mitigate the issue.

They then *contextualize* the problem through research, ascertaining its history, key players, related legislation, etc. Once they have this context, they *organize* for action, making to-do lists, dividing tasks, and planning for the next step, *action*, in which they implement their project, be that creating a PSA, hosting an informative event, or meeting with leaders. Finally, they *reflect* on their work both individually and with their group (if projects are done in groups, which we recommend) and determine next steps for action. This portion is highly significant so that students discern the ongoing nature of making change rather than thinking they are supposed to resolve a huge issue with just one project. We want them to feel successful in their action but to realize that systems of oppression are far reaching and require diligent work for transformation. Thus while we provide suggestions in each chapter, we find students are often much more imaginative and that they know what would be best in their communities. We encourage teachers to trust them to generate and implement their ideas.

Teachers can assess students at each phase of the process, interject mini-lessons as needed (e.g., on conducting research or on writing for when students might contact authority figures), and monitor progress through daily participation points and conferences. While this may feel messy, as different groups may be working on different projects, keeping students to a timeline and allowing for project work-time interspersed with whole-class instruction on the novel, or another text, can make it more manageable.

Finally, we intentionally chose diverse writers and narratives, wishing to reflect content and voices that will speak to the students in our classrooms as well as to the array of themes debated daily in society. While we have carefully selected texts that we feel authentically reflect the social topic of focus and will maintain students' interests, we understand that classroom teachers often lack access to resources/texts and the time needed to keep up with the growing field of young adult literature. Therefore, the sorts of action projects we propose can be used with a multitude of texts—our chosen book serving as an example and inspiration for teachers to make their own text and pedagogical selections.

CONSIDERATIONS FOR PRACTICE

Building a Classroom Community

Before we progress to the chapters, we feel it is necessary to include a few aspects of teaching that are crucial to the sort of pedagogies we advance. In particular, talking about social justice issues can (and should) lead to some discomfort in the classroom. As Love and Muhammad (2017) state, "Talking about race and racism among people of diverse histories and identities can be challenging and uncomfortable for some who do not have to experience racism daily; yet it is at this point where we begin to advance in knowledge, understanding, and practices" (p. 3), and we would add this extends to topics such as gender, sexuality, and nationality—all of which we cover in this book.

Beginning on the first day of school, teachers should cultivate a classroom community in which students respect one another and value others' input while expecting to be intellectually challenged. This starts with simply getting to know one another, and there are a host of ways of doing so, ranging from having students pair up and answer a series of questions about one another in a visual presentation (Abla, 2022) to an activity in which they find a classmate with a particular experience or characteristic on a list and therefore build common ties (Bucknam, 2021). Students can also engage in writing their own missions or ground rules for a class as a community (for ideas for doing this, see Ferlazzo & Denti, 2016). These can include what should happen if a student veers from these expectations as well.

A Culture of Discussion

As part of this cultivation of community, norms, and guidelines for discussion will be essential to diving into the sort of curriculum we propose in this text. Learning for Justice (2020) has a useful resource for facilitating critical conversations with students that we highly recommend. It begins with the teacher's reflection on their own levels of comfort and their feelings about their own preparation to lead potentially difficult conversations. It also includes activities for before, during, and after these sorts of discussions. The authors advise, similar to the above, establishing community agreements with students regarding the language they use, such as a community agreement could include statements like "'Listen with respect to the experiences of others,'" "'Try to understand what someone is saying before rushing to judgment'" or "'Put-downs of any kind are never OK'" (p. 12). As teachers with whom we have worked often express concerns about navigating students' emotions and worry about dialogue getting "too heated," we find these resources attending to students' emotions invaluable.

Facing History (2009) similarly purports effective strategies for leading classroom discussions particularly pertaining to race, and they propose "contracting" which is "the process of openly discussing with your students expectations about how classroom members will treat each other" (para. 1). One lesson included in this unit exposes students to concepts such as systems of oppression and to understanding why language matters so much in critical dialogue (Facing History, 2016). Finally, Singleton and Hays (2008) outline strategies for discussion that we have found useful with our own students and could easily be adapted to the middle school context. Their four guidelines are: stay engaged, expect to experience discomfort, speak your truth, and expect and accept a lack of closure. This last point can be especially trying for individuals involved (particularly youth) but this is why facing it in advance can help mitigate disappointment or negative feelings.

Addressing 'Controversy'

Often, as teachers of English Language Arts, we are faced with what are considered "controversial texts." We want to challenge this framing in our book and likewise to invite teachers to reconsider this narrative. We ask: *Who deems certain texts controversial? Why are those seen as controversial? When stakeholders (parents, administrators, etc.) claim to be protecting children, which children are they protecting, and from what?* (Beach et al, 2022; Crawley, 2020).

We think answering these questions opens space for educators to unpack the ways that book challenges and censorship can serve to perpetuate silence, oppression, and negative stereotypes. Half of the American Library Association's Banned Book List for 2021 contained books that were challenged for LGBTQIA+ content. We cannot help but ask what message this sends youth who identify on this spectrum and how it thus promotes cisgender identities and heterosexism as the norm. The National Council of Teachers of English (2018) contains a statement on The Student's Right to Read that can help support teachers' decisions as well as a form that can be used if a stakeholder wishes to challenge a text. Perhaps most important to remember is that a guardian can generally ask that their student be provided an alternate text, but they should not be allowed to remove a text for *all* students.

In addition, what and how we frame controversy for students is just as important. Hess and McAvoy (2012) provide insights for teachers to differentiate between partisan (a party affiliation such as Democrat or Republican) and political (an issue in the public). In order for students to be participants in our society, they need to engage in political discussions in which they listen to others, weigh information, and enact civil discourse. Perhaps one of the most useful points from their work is their defining "open" versus "settled" explaining, "The difference between a settled and open issue is whether it is a matter of controversy or has been decided. Settled issues are questions for which there is broad based agreement that a particular decision is well warranted. Open questions, on the other hand, are those that are matters of live controversy" (p. 161). They further note, "We suggest that there are some issues that are settled and should be taught as settled and to not do that is being dishonest with young people. For example, the question about whether climate change is occurring—that's a settled issue. The question is: What to do about climate change? That's an open issue" (Drummond, 2015, para. 15).

Conceptualizing issues in this way is advantageous to teachers when determining what should be allowed to be argued in a classroom and what should not. If a matter has been decided in a court of law (e.g., marriage equality), it should not be proposed as controversial. We would add that issues that relate to human rights are part of the category that should not be open in classrooms. Sharing this with students in advance can help facilitate respectful conversations.

Teacher Discretion, Fear, and Courage

Having been middle and high school teachers ourselves (and continuing to work in schools in various ways), we realize that each context is different. Geography, student demographics, and administration are just some of the factors that can influence curriculum and teaching. In addition, some students may be ready to discuss certain topics but not others, some topics may be too triggering depending on local events, and educators may feel underprepared or unable to raise issues for personal reasons. We firmly believe that teachers are professionals and should proceed as such; you know yourself, your students, community, and district policies best. We suggest starting with topics and texts with which you feel you have knowledge and are ready to broach and then working your way into others.

There is often a certain fear in addressing social topics in classrooms. Backlash from parents, administrators, and other stakeholders is real, and we do not wish to diminish that. As referenced above, censorship and book banning are rampant in the United States currently, and politicians seem to have more and more influence over what is being taught in classrooms. We understand that and validate this reality. However, we also caution teachers to spend time in reflection on what and who are being harmed when certain perspectives are omitted from the classroom. We, thus, want to inspire teachers to have courage. Think about whom you are fighting for when you include LGBTQIA+ topics or address Black Lives Matter. Consider that teaching about refugees and immigrants is a human rights issue. If doubt creeps in or if stakeholders question your decisions, reminding yourself of these points can restore your confidence and resolve. Finding like-minded colleagues and supporting one another's work or teaching as partners can also mitigate feelings of isolation and distress.

We also firmly suggest two strategies to alleviate possible challenges and fears: being transparent and relying on standards. Many parents actually just want to know what is happening in their student's classroom and what the teacher's rationale is for texts and projects (Boyd & Darragh, 2019c). A letter home (or provided to administration) at the beginning of the year, or at the start of a unit, explaining your approach can ward off caretakers who might misunderstand or only hear part of a novel or topic. Even if teachers do not send a letter home, having a rationale prepared (Smagorinsky, 2007) if questions arise demonstrates that your unit has purpose and careful thought. This leads to our second strategy, which is ensuring that your unit is connected to the standards to which you are held accountable. We recognize and affirm that standards can be problematic, especially when translated as the driving force for curriculum, but we are also pedagogical realists (Dyches & Sams, 2018) and know well the realities of schools. Thus, articulating a unit of study and social action projects with the literacy standards they accomplish can be crucial. And social justice does not happen at the sacrifice of skills and knowledge (Cochran-Smith et al., 2009; Golden, 2008). Rather, those are acquired when students are more motivated to learn them because they are reading about and exploring in their areas of interest. Dover (2015), for example, illustrated how "Twenty-four secondary ELA teachers, representing thirteen US states" (p. 520) achieved Common Core State Standards for literacy while simultaneously teaching about a variety of social justice topics. Many "saw literature analysis as an opportunity to engage students in thinking critically about issues of equity and justice," and using those that did so "required students to use close reading, draw inferences, or cite specific textual evidence" (p. 521). Thus, it is entirely possible to draw upon your standards to justify teaching the novels and topics we propose.

This book proposes myriad ways that teachers can encourage students to read and act in the moment. It is, of course, our hope that this will produce students who carry equity-related work over into their adult lives as participants in our democracy, but our focus is on the readers present within the classroom space. Middle-level readers are at a transformative point in their cognitive and social development, entering middle school as children and leaving as young adults. We feel this time is crucial for young readers to be given opportunity, power, and agency to explore social issues in their communities and around the world and to take action to address them. Youth can be quite discerning and creative when provided a platform to do so. We hope that the pages that follow will inspire teachers to offer that very space.

REFERENCES

Abla, C. (2022). The first 5 days: The key to success. *Edutopia*. https://www.edutopia.org/article/first-5-days-key-success

Banned & Challenged Books. (2022). Top 10 most challenged book lists. A website of the ALA Office for Intellectual Freedom. https://www.ala.org/advocacy/bbooks/frequentlychallengedbooks/top10

Beach, R., Boyd, A., Webb, A., & Thein, A. (2022). *Teaching to exceed English Language Arts Standards: A critical inquiry approach for 6–12 classroom* (3rd ed.). Routledge.

Blackburn, M. V., & Clark, C. T. (2011). Analyzing talk in a long-term literature discussion group: Ways of operating within LGBT-inclusive and queer discourses. *Reading Research Quarterly, 46*, 222–248.

Boyd, A. (2017). *Social justice literacies in the English classroom: Teaching practice in action.* Teachers College Press.

Boyd, A. & Bereiter, T. (2017). "I don't really know what a fair portrayal is and what a stereotype is": Pluralizing transgender narratives with young adult literature. *English Journal, 107*(1), 13–18.

Boyd, A. & Darragh, J. (2019a). *Reading for action: Engaging youth in social justice through Young Adult Literature.* Rowman & Littlefield.

Boyd, A. & Darragh, J. (2019b). Critical literacies on the university campus: Engaging pre-service teachers with social action projects. *English Teaching: Practice & Critique, 19*(1), 49–63.

Boyd, A. & Darragh, J. (2019c). Complicating censorship: Reading *All American Boys* with parents of young adults. *English Education, 51*(3), 229–260.

Boyd, A. & Miller, J. (2020). Let's give them something to talk (and act!) about: Privilege, racism, and oppression in the middle school classroom. *Voices from the Middle, 27*(3), 15–19.

Bucknam, S. (2021). Ten middle-school ice breakers to get your students talking. *Teaching Expertise.* https://www.teachingexpertise.com/classroom-ideas/middle-school-ice-breakers/

Canadian Teachers' Federation & The Critical Thinking Consortium. (2010). Social action projects: Making a difference K-4. Ottawa, ON: Canadian Teachers Federation and The Critical Thinking Consortium.

Chang, B., Lavergne, A., Pinkerton, K., Ripp, P., Silveri, G. (2018). The students' right to read. National Council of Teachers of English. https://ncte.org/statement/righttoreadguideline/

Cochran-Smith, M., Barnatt, J., Lahann, R., Shakman, K., & Terrell, D. (2009). Teacher education for social justice: Critiquing the critiques. In W. Ayers, T. Quinn, & D. Stovall (Eds.), *Handbook of social justice in education* (pp. 625–639). Routledge.

Crawley, S. A. (2020). "The sky didn't fall or anything": A mother's response to lesbian and gay-inclusive picture books in elementary schools in the United States. *Bookbird,* 58(1), 29–44.

Dover, A. (2015). Teaching for social justice and the common core: Justice-oriented curriculum for language arts and literacy. *Journal of Adolescent and Adult Literacy, 59*(5), 517–527.

Drummond, S. (2015). Politics in the classroom: How much is too much? nprED. https://www.npr.org/sections/ed/2015/12/16/459673575/politics-in-the-classroom-how-much-is-too-much.

Durand, E. S., & Jiménez-García, M. (2018). Unsettling representations of identities: A critical review of diverse youth literature. *Research on Diversity in Youth Literature, 1*(1), 7.

Dyches, J. & Sams, B. (2018). Reconciling competing missions of English education: A story of pedagogical realism. *Changing English.* https://www.tandfonline.com/doi/abs/10.1080/1358684X.2018.1499006

Elish-Piper, Coffey, H. & Fulton, S. (2018). The responsible change project: Building a justice- oriented middle school curriculum through critical service-learning. *Middle School Journal, 49*(5), 16–25.

Facing History & Ourselves. (2009). Contracting. https://www.facinghistory.org/resource-library/contracting-0

Facing History & Ourselves. (2016). Preparing students for difficult conversations. https://www.facinghistory.org/resource-library/preparing-students-difficult-conversations#preparing-to-teach

Fairclough, N. (2015). *Language and power* (3rd ed.). Routledge.

Ferlazzo, L. & Denti, L. (2016). Response: Classroom rules—ways to create, introduce, and reinforce them. *Education Week*. https://www.edweek.org/teaching-learning/opinion-response-classroom-rules-ways-to-create-introduce-enforce-them/2016/06

Glenn, W. (2012). Developing understandings of race: Preservice teachers' counter-narrative (re) constructions of people of color in young adult literature. *English Education, 44*(4), 326–353.

Golden, J. (2008). A conversation with Linda Christensen on social justice education. *English Journal, 97*(6), 59–64.

Hess, D. E., & McAvoy, P. (2012). *The political classroom: Evidence and ethics in democratic education*. Routledge.

Learning for Justice (2020). Let's talk: Facilitating critical conversations with students. Teaching Tolerance. https://www.learningforjustice.org/sites/default/files/2021-01/TT-Let-s-Talk-Publication-January-2020.pdf.

Miller, M. E. (2014). The power of conversation: Linking discussion of social justice to literacy standards. *Voices from the Middle, 22*(1), 36–42.

Rezvi, S. Han, H. Larnell, G. V. (2020). Mathematical mirrors, windows, and sliding glass doors: Young adult texts as sites for identifying with mathematics. *Journal of Adolescent & Adult Literacy, 63*(5), 589–592.

Sciurba, K. (2014). Texts as mirrors, texts as windows. *Journal of Adolescent & Adult Literacy, 58*(4), 308–316.

Sims Bishop, R. (1990). Mirrors, windows, and sliding glass doors. *Perspectives, 6*(3), ix–xi.

Singleton, G., & Hays, C. (2008). Beginning courageous conversations about race. In M. Pollock (Ed.). *Everyday antiracism: Getting real about race in school* (pp. 18–23). The New Press.

Smagorinsky, P. (2007). *Teaching English by design: How to create and carry out instructional units*. Heinemann.

Stachowiak, D. M. (2017). Social action and social justice: A path to critical consciousness for engagement. *Voices from the Middle, 24*(3), 29–32.

Chapter 1

Coping With Trauma

According to the United States Department of Health and Human Services (2022), two-thirds of children will have experienced a traumatic event by the time they are sixteen years old. Traumas may be related to abuse, neglect, sudden loss of a loved one, natural disaster, physical or sexual assault, life-threatening accidents or illness, or witnessing domestic violence, among other factors. With the prevalence of trauma, it is important for teachers to help students understand what trauma is, how it can affect learning and daily life, and the resources to manage it. Indeed, trauma can be a result of many of the topics we will center on in other chapters of this book including bullying, disability, poverty, immigration, refugeeism, and living in foster care and is why we intentionally begin this text with the topic. This chapter will describe an experience with trauma by focusing on the novel *Ghost,* the first book in the *Track* series by Jason Reynolds. Intersections with bullying, race, and social class arise while Castle, the main character, manages the trauma from his past, and are thus central elements for focus in discussion and learning activities. As so many students will most likely have experiences with trauma already, this chapter will focus on managing and coping with trauma in order to support mental health as well as ways in which to support others who may be living with trauma through the creation of social action projects.

GHOST

The first book of the *Track* series, *Ghost* by Jason Reynolds (2016), shares the narrative of Castle "Ghost," the newest member of the elite track team, the Defenders. Readers learn that previously, Castle's father chased him and his mother with a loaded gun, attempting to kill them. They ran to the local market, where they hid in Mr. Charles's storage closet. Castle struggles with getting into trouble at school, where he is bullied for where he lives and how he dresses, both due to the family's lack of income. His mother is studying to be a nurse and works at a hospital, a benefit of which she can bring home food from the cafeteria each night for her and Castle to eat. Struggling to cope and getting into trouble, Castle is discovered by Coach Brody, a track coach who grew up in the same neighborhood and under similar circumstances with regards to an unsupportive father and lack of income. Coach Brody convinces Castle to join his elite track team and supports the seventh grader in his journey to do well in school and stay the course for success in his life. The novel ends with Castle on the starting line for the one-hundred-meter dash in his first track meet as a member of the Defenders.

TEACHING STRATEGIES

Before Reading

Before reading, teachers might want to provide an overview of what trauma is and how it can affect the brain and being successful in school. Teachers might want to invite the school counselor or psychologist in, or local therapists who have expertise in discussing trauma with youth. According to the NCTSN (National Child Traumatic Stress Network), trauma is "The physical and emotional responses of a child to events that threaten the life or physical or emotional wellness of the child, or of someone critically important to the child" (para 2). These can be one-time events (acute trauma) or chronic, complex traumas—repeated incidents that over time cause unhealthy stress levels. Based on a study by the CDC and Kaiser (Centers for Disease Control and Prevention, n.d.) these ongoing experiences are called ACEs (Adverse Childhood Experiences) and the more ACEs a child experiences, the more likely they are to struggle with learning, memory, social skills, behavior regulation, and with their physical, mental, and emotional health. Teachers might want to introduce what are considered ACEs:

- Emotional, physical, or sexual abuse
- Emotional or physical neglect
- Witnessing violence against one's mother
- A parent's addiction to alcohol or other substance, or a family member's mental illness
- Separation or divorce
- The incarceration of a parent
- Involvement with the foster care system
- Witnessing community violence
- Living in an unsafe neighborhood
- Bullying

- Experiencing racism (CDC, Fast facts, n.d.)

In doing so, however, teachers should remind students that experiencing trauma is, unfortunately, quite normal (one in four children has experienced more than one ACE), and that having been exposed to trauma does NOT mean that youth will necessarily struggle academically, socially, and emotionally in and out of school. Rather, in identifying what causes trauma, how it can impact the brain, and ways in which to manage and combat trauma, students can heal. Moreover, teachers should focus on the resilience and strengths of all students in the classroom, in spite of the traumas they have experienced.

After explaining what trauma is, teachers might want to address how trauma can affect the brain. There are several short videos that can be helpful in explaining these difficult concepts. For example, the UK Trauma Council's short YouTube video, "Childhood Trauma and the Brain" can shed light on how trauma can impact everyday life, and how we can support those who have experienced childhood trauma. Explaining the different parts of the brain and how they function is the brief video "Trauma and the Brain" (Dovetail Qld, 2019). Giving students information about biology and brain development and how trauma and stress can impact brain development and processing can be helpful for all students to better understand the impacts of trauma. Teachers might also want to share with students the concept of "Upstairs and Downstairs Brain" (Momentous Institute, 2019). This simple visual analogy of the brain shows students that the lower part of the brain is responsible for basic life functioning, while the upper part of the brain is responsible for higher order thinking, memory, attention, and behavior regulation. When students are stressed, it is physiologically challenging for them to access the "upstairs" part of their brain. It can be helpful for students to understand and to be able to identify when they are not able to engage their "upstairs brain" due to their strong emotions and to know that this lack of access will impact their abilities to think critically and rationally. The Momentous Institute provides some resources for teachers who want to learn more about this analogy and how to use it with youth. A quick internet search of "upstairs and downstairs brain" will also yield multiple resources on this topic, including some short videos like SEL Sketches' (2021) "Upstairs Brain Downstairs Brain" and Momentous Institute's (2022) "The Upstairs and Down-stairs Brain with Dr. Tina Payne Bryson." Again, in all cases teachers should make sure not to use a deficit perspective when talking about the impacts of trauma, emotion regulation, and neuroplasticity; the focus should be on healing, recovery, and hope.

During Reading

From the very start of the novel, we learn that Castle loves reading the *Guinness Book of World Records* and sharing with his family and friends all of the unique records that have been made. Students might look up various world records and then present on one they have found that seems the most interesting to them. In addition, they could identify which record they personally would like to hold and explain why. Teachers can lead students in thinking deeply about records in general, asking questions like: *Why do you think records exist? Why do people want to break records that exist/ hold current records? What can be gained by holding a record?* Once students have identified that being the best at something can make them feel good/positively impact their self-esteem, teachers might encourage students to come up with their own *Book of Class Records*, where they can identify a strength of each person in the class. They might, for example, identify the best encourager in the class, the best jokester, the best at sharing, etc. Afterwards, they might want to think of other things that can also make them feel good about themselves, things that might be easier to achieve, like conducting random acts of kindness or listening to a favorite song and having an impromptu dance party.

In the first chapter, readers find out about Castle's father and his resulting trauma. Castle explains:

> It was three years ago when my dad lost it. When the liquor made him meaner than he'd ever been. Every other night he would become a different person, like, he'd morph into someone crazy, but this one night my mother decided to finally fight back. This one night everything went worse . . . my dad fired a shot. He was shooting at us! My dad! *My* dad was actually shooting . . . at . . . US! His wife and his boy! (pp. 5–6)

Teachers might take this opportunity to talk about how substance abuse can cause people to "become a different person," and how it is not the victim's fault, even if the person under the influence purports it to be. They might also take this time to talk about how sometimes people we love do bad things. And it is ok to love parts of a person, but not other parts of them, or to love them, but not their actions. Later Castle explains, "They gave him ten years in prison, and to be honest, I don't know if I'm happy about that or not. Sometimes I wish he would've gotten forever in jail. Other times, I wish he was home on the couch, watching the game, shaking seeds in his hand" (p. 7). Again, teachers might take this opportunity to talk about the complexity of people and relationships. They might guide students in identifying characters in television shows, films, books, or comic books who demonstrate qualities that can be admired and qualities that can be abhorred. They might consider this quote from George Martin, whose fantasy novels inspired the television series *Game of Thrones,* "As Faulkner says, all of us have the capacity in us for great good and for great evil, for love but also for hate. I wanted to write those kinds of complex characters in a fantasy, and not just have all the good people get together to fight the bad guy." Teachers can ask students what they think this quote means, if they agree with it, and what effects complex characters can have on readers and viewers. They might even try creating their own complex character sketches, indicating both the "good" and the "bad" their character possesses and ultimately how they can use their good to fight the evil within themselves.

Throughout the novel, Castle can be seen buying and eating sunflower seeds. He even eats less at lunch so he will have a dollar to buy from Mr. Charles's store each day. Students can make a list of their favorite snack foods. They might do some research to analyze the nutritional value of their choices. Then they might investigate what makes them like that particular snack and if it is something that is good or bad for their health. For example, students might identify liking energy drinks or sugary treats because they make them awake and excited. They might then research the effects of too much sugar and caffeine on the body and try to identify other, healthier and more sustaining options. Conversely, they might identify that a snack is their favorite because they have it on a special occasion or because someone important to them makes it. They might try to figure out how they can make that treat or something similar on their own. In this case, the focus should be on *feelings* and healthy choices we can make that will bring us small moments of joy. The snacks identified could eventually be put into a class cookbook, with visuals and descriptive/narrative essays explaining the importance of the food to individual students.

When Castle and his mother escape in the night, they find refuge in the storage room at Mr. Charles's store, and throughout the novel, Mr. Charles is a sort of father figure and a safe person and place for Castle. Similarly, Castle's mom, Coach Brody, and Aunt Sophie are positive, supportive, stable adults in his life. Teachers might guide students in identifying who their "safe" people and places are. Research shows that the number one thing that can ignite neuroplasticity, the brain's ability to rewire itself and reduce the effects of trauma, is having a safe, stable adult in a child's life. In having students think through their "safe" people and spaces, teachers are giving students tools to combat the trauma they might be experiencing. If teachers are comfortable, they might share with students that they are happy to be one of the "safe" people on their lists, and they hope the school will be a safe place as well.

Castle describes himself as having "a lot of scream inside" (p. 34). Teachers can guide students in discussing what this means. *What does it mean to have scream inside you? What other feelings can you identify as having inside? How do you feel when you have a lot of scream inside you? What do you want to do? What could you do to deal with the scream in healthy ways? What are some ways we can make that scream go away?* Again, helping students to identify their feelings is a trauma-sensitive teaching technique, and teachers can explicitly explain to students that being able to identify and name their emotions is the first step in being able to manage them. As a follow up, teachers can share with students some deep-breathing techniques that also might help them to manage the "scream" or other emotions, anxieties, and stresses they may be having difficulties regulating. A quick internet search will yield numerous results from simple explanations of the technique to short videos that guide students through the breathing exercise (e.g., Adolescent Wellness; Mindfulness for Teens and Adults, 2018). Teachers might guide students through a breathing exercise each day at the beginning of the class. This is a quick way to set the stage for learning, and it can be beneficial not only for students in the classroom but for teachers as well. Teachers might also want to help students identify under what circumstances they may want to try using breathing methods in their lives outside of school.

When Coach Brody takes the "newbies" out to dinner, he tells them that they have to "tell everybody one thing about yourself that most people don't know. Something good" (p. 126). In response, each of the five new members of the track team shares something with the group. The examples they share are all pretty personal, and teachers could emulate this activity but include that students don't have to share things they are uncomfortable sharing. But they can share something positive about themselves that others might not know, like "I am a good big brother. I babysit my siblings every day after school." This is a way to help create and strengthen classroom community and to also provide space for students to focus on the positive qualities they possess and to share those with others.

After Reading

As this novel focuses on trauma, stress, and managing emotions, teachers might want to invite a school counselor, school psychologist, or counselors in the community to speak about these topics. Following, students might be encouraged to research coping mechanisms and to adopt healthy outlets for stress, practicing them as a class. In order to act on their understandings, students might host a community night on self-care, undertake a campaign against bullying, and/or advertise local resources for mental health services.

The novel mentions athletes like LeBron James and Usain Bolt. Even Coach Brody was an Olympian. Students might want to research an athlete from a sport they like and share that information with the class. Moreover, they might specifically research how that favorite athlete manages stress and their overall mental health. For example, Naomi Osaka, Serena Williams, Usain Bolt, Michael Phelps, and Simone Biles have all been outspoken regarding their mental health. Students can read about these athletes in general and what they have shared regarding managing stress and their mental health and share what they have learned with the class through a multimedia presentation or in informal class discussions.

Ghost and his mom often spend evenings watching his mom's favorite movies. Students might make a list of their favorite feel good/comfort movies, and then identify patterns and themes among them. *What characteristics do their favorite movies share? What about these movies makes them happy?* They can then go one step farther and create a class movie-review guide to share with their classmates, school, or even the community, indicating things like "What to watch if you want to laugh," "What to watch if you want to have a good cry," "What to watch if you want to escape reality," and "What to watch if you want a happy ending." Again, activities like this can help students better identify their emotional needs and healthy ways to manage their feelings.

In a climactic moment in the novel, Coach Brody confronts Castle about stealing a pair of running shoes. Castle claims that Coach doesn't understand what his life is like, to which Coach responds: "I know what it's like to live here. I know what it's like to be angry, to feel, I don't know, rage on the inside . . . And the same thing running did for me, I felt like it could do for you . . . Show you that you can't run away from who you are but what you can do is run toward who you want to be" (p. 155). Teachers can help students to unpack this line of the book by asking questions like: *What does it mean that you can't run away from who you are? What does it mean that you can run toward who you want to be? Who DO you want to be? What are the steps it will take to get there? What is one thing you can do TODAY to make that come true? What is something you can do next week, next month, next year?* Teachers can then lead students in goal-setting activities with both short- and long-term goals that they can refer back to each week and track their progress.

Finally, the book ends with a cliffhanger; the starting gun has gone off at the beginning of Ghost's first-ever race—the one-hundred-meter dash. Teachers might have students write the next chapter of the book. They can then share these and vote on which ending they like best. The teacher then might share the beginning of the second book in the series, *Patina,* and let students see how closely their chosen endings match the one the author created.

INTERSECTIONS

This novel has clear intersections with bullying and poverty. Castle shares, "I was used to people treating me funny. When your clothes are two sizes too big, and you got on no-name sneakers, and your mother cuts your hair and it looks like your mother cuts your hair, you get used to people treating you funny" (p. 24). Teachers might refer to activities mentioned in Chapter 3 that focus on bullying and ways to combat it in their schools and communities.

Poverty is another intersection in the book. Ghost rations what he eats at lunch, so he has a dollar for sunflower seeds. He runs in long pants and high tops, which he later cuts off, because he doesn't have athletic clothing or shoes to wear, and he doesn't want to ask his mother for money to buy these things. Castle also mentions the "gross but free meal we were going to be having for dinner" (p. 26). Teachers might lead students in considering questions like: *Why do people bully others based on what they have and don't have? What can we do if we see someone bullying someone else? How can we help others to get the items they need?* Throughout the book, Castle often mentions food. Teachers might lead students in researching the costs of food in their local grocery store, cafeteria, farmers' market, and restaurants. They can compare the cost of foods and investigate how much healthy foods cost compared to unhealthy foods, for example, considering why this may be, and what they might be able to do as an actionable response.

IDEAS FOR SOCIAL ACTION

Running is a safe outlet for Castle and a way for him to manage his trauma and stress. The arts can also provide a safe outlet for healing. Students might take an inventory of the safe outlets their schools and communities provide. If they find something to be lacking (e.g., there is no school track team or local running club), they can consider starting their own, researching what they would need to get a running club going as well as how to advertise and recruit members. Similar projects could center around the arts and provide opportunities for children and teens to participate in the arts outside of the school day. Similarly, in reflecting on Castle's lack of athletic equipment, students might look into the costs of participating on sports teams both in and out of school. They might look to see if scholarships or other financial supports are available and ways to get this information to students who might like to join. Further, they could hold an athletic clothes and shoes drive and create a place in their school where students who would like to participate in sports can have access to the appropriate sporting gear, be it clothing, shoes, baseball mitts, etc.

Using the list of feel-good movies and the snack list they created from the above activities, students might host a movie night for their friends, family, and community members. They could share some information about taking care of mental health and accept donations to be contributed to the organization of their choice that supports youth. In conjunction with a project like that, students could create their own "Are You Ok?" (Cannon, 2021) short film using software such as Animoto and modeling after the animated short, inspiring classmates and younger children to reach out to each other, check in with each other, and fight against those who may try to make others feel bad or less than. A video like this could be screened during the previews of their movie night.

Finally, Coach Brody was in the Olympics, and this sporting event might inspire students to create their own Olympics. They could organize games, create prizes, and invite elementary age students or perhaps students receiving disability services to participate. They could advertise the event and perhaps take donations from spectators and/or sell refreshments and then donate that money to the charity of their choice.

Trauma is something that affects so many people, and learning how to manage and heal from trauma can be a life-changing skill. In focusing on social emotional and mental health along with healthy outlets for managing stress, a unit centered on trauma with a novel like *Ghost* can benefit students outside of the English classroom and into their futures.

SUPPLEMENTAL RESOURCES

Connected Young Adult Literature

Mosquitoland by David Arnold
Hey, Kiddo by Jarrett Krosoczka
Patina (#2 in the *Track* series) by Jason Reynolds
Sunny (#3 in the *Track* series) by Jason Reynolds
Lu (#4 in the *Track* series) by Jason Reynolds
The List of Things that Will Not Change by Rebecca Stead

Connected Music

"This Is Me" by Keala Settle and *The Greatest Showman* ensemble
"Scars" by Allison Iraheta
"A Little's Enough" by Angels and Airwaves
"Fight Song" by Rachel Platten

"Flames" by David Guetta and Sia

Connected Videos

Canon, R., Director. (2021). Are You Okay? https://www.youtube.com/watch?v=tJsGGsPNakw

Dovetail Qld. (2019). Trauma and the Brain. https://www.youtube.com/watch?v=ZLF_SEy6sdc

Momentous Institute. (2022). The Upstairs Brain with Dr. Tina Payne Bryson. https://www.youtube.com/watch?v=Hgw_BQ442HU

SEL Sketches. (2021). Upstairs Brain Downstairs Brain. https://www.youtube.com/watch?v=dk1Nt-xnSGI

Connected Breathing Resources

Adolescent Wellness. (n.d.). Deep Breathing Exercises. https://www.adolescentwellness.org/wp-content/uploads/2011/06/Relaxation_Exercises_for_Adolescents_and_Adults.pdf

Coping Skills for Kids. (2021). Deep Breathing Exercises for Kids. https://copingskillsforkids.com/deep-breathing-exercises-for-kids

Mindfulness for Teens and Adults. (2019). 4-7-8 Breathing Exercises to Alleviate Anxiety and Stress for Teens and Adults. https://www.youtube.com/watch?v=PmBYdfv5RSk

Connected Texts on Trauma Sensitive Teaching

Dutro, E. (2019). *The vulnerable heart: Centering trauma as powerful pedagogy.* Teachers College Press.

Jennings, P. A. (2019). *The trauma-sensitive classroom: Building resilience with compassionate teaching.* W. W. Norton and Company.

Zacarian, D., Alvarez-Ortiz, L., & Haynes, J. (2017). *Teaching to strengths: Supporting students living with trauma, violence, and chronic stress.* ASCD.

REFERENCES

Centers for Disease Control and Prevention (n.d.). About the CDC-Kaiser ACE Study. https://www.cdc.gov/violenceprevention/aces/about.html

Momentous Institute. (2019). Upstairs and downstairs brain. https://momentousinstitute.org/blog/upstairs-and-downstairs-brain

National Child Traumatic Stress Network. (n.d.). About childhood trauma. https://www.nctsn.org/what-is-child-trauma/about-child-trauma

SEL Sketches. (2021). Upstairs brain downstairs brain. https://www.youtube.com/watch?v=dk1Nt-xnSGI

UK Trauma Council. (2020). Childhood trauma and the brain. https://www.youtube.com/watch?v=xYBUY1kZpf8

U.S. Department of Health and Human Services. (2022). Understanding childhood trauma. Substance Abuse and Mental Health Services Administration (SAMHSA). https://www.samhsa.gov/child-trauma/understanding-child-trauma#:~:text=Child%20trauma%20occurs%20more%20than,Psychological%2C%20physical%2C%20or%20sexual%20abuse

Chapter 2

Social Class Disparities in the United States

Social class disparities have increased in the United States over the past five decades. Since 1971, there has been a "shrinking of the middle class" that "has been accompanied by an increase in the share of adults in the upper-income tier—from 14% in 1971 to 21% in 2021—as well as an increase in the share of who are in the lower-income tier, from 25% to 29%" (Kochhar & Sechopoulos, 2022, para 2). This wide gap between those with more income and resources and those with less is experienced across all aspects of daily life—from schooling to health care to recreation. People with greater access to resources have more options for housing and jobs as well as more opportunities for advanced education and travel. This problem is exacerbated by generational wealth, or "any kind of asset that families pass down to their children or grandchildren, whether in the form of cash, investment funds, stocks and bonds, properties, or even entire companies" (Matteo, 2022, para. 7). This creates a cycle of who remains wealthy and who does not, which is difficult to break. Social class disparities are thus a systemic issue that needs to be addressed with students so that they can better grasp the effects of such inequity and can envision ways to effect change.

The United States Census Bureau defines "poverty thresholds" by size of family and number of children. For example, in 2021, for a household with two people under the age of sixty-five and one child the threshold was $18,608. In 2015, the US Department of Agriculture reported that "a family will spend approximately $12,980 annually per child in a middle-income . . . family" (Lino, 2020, para. 2). This difference is stark and illustrates the profound divide in income and need in this country. Meanwhile, the stigma around those with limited access persists, and narratives of blame on individuals are rampant. Politicians and other public figures speak out about a lack of desire to work or money spent unwisely and worry that government assistance induces laziness and causes dependence. Opposition, however, notes minimum wage is not livable in many states (with the federal minimum wage set at $7.25/hour) and does not cover basic expenses (Waddell, 2021) or discern how issues compound. A person without an income, for instance, does not have access to quality health care, which can cause an inability to work.

Thus issues related to income and social classes are complicated. While students are likely to be familiar with the concept of poverty and either have personal experiences or know someone who is struggling financially, this chapter will encourage students to explore how poverty affects individuals in the United States. Using *The Benefits of Being an Octopus* (Braden, 2018) as a focal text, this chapter will guide teachers in helping students to explore systemic poverty and the ways in which having a limited income and accessing available resources impacts various facets of everyday life.

THE BENEFITS OF BEING AN OCTOPUS

Zoey, the protagonist in Ann Braden's (2018) *The Benefits of Being an Octopus*, is a girl in the seventh grade living with her mom, her three younger siblings, her mother's boyfriend, Lenny, and his father. The kids share one room in Lenny's trailer which is described as an upgrade from their previous living conditions. Zoey shares at the beginning of the novel that they "moved four times over the course" of one year (p. 3) and at one point lived in their car. The novel follows Zoey's journey as she attends school and is encouraged by her teacher to join the debate club but struggles with bullying and kids whose worlds (and accompanying privileges) are far from her own. She cares for her younger brother and sister daily, meeting them at the bus stop after school, watching them while her mom is at work, and conducting dinner and bedtime routines.

As the story progresses, readers are exposed to the verbal abuse Zoey's mother, Kara, experiences from Lenny. He demeans her abilities constantly, makes her question herself, and expects her gratitude for his care for her and her family. Meanwhile, Zoey remembers her mother from before she met Lenny and refers often to her "old, competent mom" (p. 73) that she misses. Eventually, and after some disappointing attempts, Zoey convinces her mother to leave Lenny. They do so in an intense scene fleeing his home, and Kara is granted a protective order from a judge and finds housing for her and her children with Zoey's best friend Fuschia and her mother.

TEACHING STRATEGIES

Before Reading

As mentioned above, it is crucial to help students understand that social class disparities occur because of systemic cycles rather than any specific choice a person makes. As such, teachers can begin this unit by defining concepts such as *generational wealth, poverty, social class, economic privilege*, and *minimum wage*. Learning for Justice (2022) offers a four-lesson sequence for middle-grades learners in which they explore the costs of living in their community; understand poverty as related to unemployment; define the cycle of poverty; and draw connections between race and poverty. One or all of these lessons would benefit students in building foundational understandings before starting the book. As this resource cautions, however, it is critical to ensure not to further stigmatize students who might experience limited access to resources and to develop the empathy for those who are more privileged.

As an activity, students could research the minimum wage in their own state and compare that to others across the country. US News and World Report's article, "Report: $15 Hourly Wage Isn't Livable Anywhere in the United States" (Waddell, 2021) has an interactive map that could help students with this research as does the U.S. Department of Labor (2022). They could brainstorm ways to appeal to local employers, state legislators, and federal officials for higher wages. Teachers can then create lists with students of everyday expenses people have that they may take for granted (power, water, food) and lead them through understanding how those prices add up and what it looks like when those are subtracted from the minimum wages they found. They could also discuss how, when a person's income is already limited and they are forced to pay extra rent or have an unexpected bill arise such as a health bill, or when a car part needs replacing, this can set them back again and again. We typically caution against simulations or privilege walk types of activities, as these are surface level and can often reinforce stereotypes. Instead, examining costs of living and unforeseen expenses as we have suggested can be constructive in helping students see how issues compound to make financial stability difficult.

Teachers might also begin the unit with a read aloud of the excerpt "The Low Cuts Strike Again," a short story from Jason Reynolds's (2019) book *Look Both Ways* about a group of kids who steal loose change out of necessity and pool their money to buy ice cream for one of the youth's mother who is undergoing chemotherapy. The story defies stereotypes of poverty and uncaring youth, addressing issues such as free lunch and health care. Teachers could use this to set the stage for Braden's (2018) novel, asking students to consider: *How does the author appeal to stereotypes in the story? What* did you think the characters were going to do with the money? How does the ending show us that the protagonist is still a child, despite having adult-like concerns?

Finally, students could view the Kristen Miale (2016) TEDx Talk "Moving Beyond Basic Needs to Break the Cycle of Poverty." In this video, the speaker discusses how attempts to address poverty ignore issues around self-esteem as well as common misconceptions around people living in poverty. She elaborates on the trauma surrounding poverty such as the lasting effects of feeling unsafe or without food. She also describes how even society's attempts to provide resources for people living without are done in ways that are shameful, providing low quality food and discarded items such as clothing. This relates well to the novel and can thus set up students for reading and understanding Zoey's story. Teachers could ask students, after watching, to journal about what they learned from the video and what they still would like to know.

During Reading

As students read the novel, they will notice there are many ways that issues related to social class arise. First, Zoey discloses her lack of material resources and her prior living conditions. She shares, "In our last apartment, pre-Lenny, the countertop was rotting around the edges, so you'd realize halfway through washing dishes that water had been pooling downstream into the carpeting. We basically spent our six months in that apartment ducking under the five clotheslines that crisscrossed the main room and smelling like we lived in a swamp" (Braden, 2018, p. 19). Later in the novel, we learn that her mom walks to the laundromat and has little room for everyone's things, so they have to be selective on what can be cleaned (p. 72) and at one point Zoey tells her friend at school, " I don't even have a phone" (p. 64). Teachers can guide students in discussing how quality of life can be impacted when one has limited income. They can ask questions like: *How can lack of resources impact a family's basic needs? How does having limited resources add more stress to one's daily life? What daily activities take longer and/or are more stressful when one does not have disposable income? How can a lack of resources impact a person's physical, mental, and emotional health? How can it impact one's sense of belonging and ability to fully participate in recreational activities, society, and life?*

Zoey frequently contrasts her situation with that of her peers at her school, such as Matt Hubbard. Matt's mom helps him remember his homework, and in one scene in the novel, he gets on the bus with a banana smoothie, which prompts Zoey to share: "I try to picture my mom pulling herself out of bed to make me a smoothie because I'm tired in the morning. As if she wasn't exhausted. As if she didn't have to take care of Hector. As if Frank wouldn't throw a fit for getting woken up by a blender. As if we had a working blender. As if we had bananas. As if" (p. 93). These small privileges that her classmates experience impact Zoey on a deep level. Later, when there is an issue with ordering carnations for the class for Valentine's Day and a group of girls says dividing them would be "the worst thing ever" (p. 183), Zoey is floored by their extreme response. She asks: "Because that's the difference, isn't it? For them, it's like an easy life is automatic, and when it's not, they're all ready to pour on righteous anger and think they can do something about it. Probably because they're armed with more than a measly Q-tip" (p. 184). Teachers can prompt students to consider: *How does Zoey's life differ from her peers? Why do you think the issues of the smoothie or the carnations are so striking to her? What privileges do her peers have that Zoey is not afforded without any of them being responsible for (earning) them?*

Almost immediately, we learn that Zoey experiences bullying and feels ashamed due to her home situation. When she gets on the bus to go to school, she is met with another girl "making noises as if a pile of rotting fish was just deposited in her lap. 'That smell,' she says. Like she always does" (p. 29). Later, Zoey says, "In our homeroom row, fancy-pants Kaylee Vine and Nellie Abbott are making eyes at my shirt like it once mugged them in a dark alley" (p. 67). Teachers could ask students to document these instances and to draw connections to Kristen Miale's points from the TEDx Talk. For instance, Zoey calls herself "grimy" (p. 48, p. 67) and considers "maybe I'm the stub of an already used bus ticket . . . and even then I'm the ticket stub that's at the back of the bus with muddy boot marks all over it" (p. 39). She has internalized the negative messages she receives at school and they have gravely affected her self confidence (see Chapter 3 on bullying). At one point, Zoey says "one of the things you know for sure is that everyone you're going up against is better than you" (p. 42), illustrating how she feels less than her peers at school. Teachers could ask: *How do Zoey's feelings about herself and her clothing relate to Miale's story about why kids in need want Nikes for Christmas? How does Zoey demonstrate the connection between basic needs being met versus a sense of belonging?*

Extending upon this, Zoey is baffled, for example, that "his [Matt's] bus stop is magically right in front of house" (p. 30) and that his family goes out for pizza "every single Saturday night. Every single one!" (p. 31). She feels that Matt lives on a "beautiful tropical island, and I can see it and smell the pizza, but no matter how hard I swim I can't get there" (p. 31) and says: "That's one of the things about people on that beautiful tropical island: they can't see who's floating about in the ocean around them. Or maybe they can and they just choose not to look. I don't know" (p. 31). Teachers can ask: *What* is Zoey calling a beautiful tropical island—how is this a metaphor? Why does she describe it as such? What is she saying here about wealthy people and their knowledge of the poor? Why does she feel unseen? To what extent is this true in our society? What are some examples from other books, television, or film that illustrate this phenomenon of people not "seeing," literally and figuratively, those who are struggling around them?*

In addition, teachers could ask students to create a T-chart and on the left side to keep a list of how Zoey's schooling is particularly affected by her financial situation. For example, she is unable to attend a field trip "to the aquarium in Boston (my mom kept 'forgetting' to send in the payment" (p. 3)) and she does not complete a school project because she does not have "glitter and markers and poster board and all sorts of things" (p. 2). She forgets her debate packet for school because she was dealing with a power outage at home from a bill not being paid. On the right side, students could then generate ways that schools could work against these limitations to help students. For instance, they could keep a fund for field trips for students who need it and they could offer a resource room for students to get supplies for projects. While free and reduced meals are widespread, these other areas are often overlooked in the costs of schooling.

Mrs. Rochambeau is a teacher who encourages Zoey to join the debate club and supports her in many ways. She tells Zoey, "only you can choose what kind of person you become" (p. 94) to which Zoey responds, "That assumes I have a choice" (p. 94). This is a crucial scene to discuss with students given their pre reading work and the focus on systemic oppression. Teachers can ask: *To what extent does Zoey have a choice in her circumstances? What are the factors that inhibit her? What decisions are within her means to change her situation? Given the cycle of poverty discussed before we read the novel, how do you think Zoey could break the cycle?*

This might prompt students to consider how difficult it is to break a social cycle. They could watch the video of Ben Tecumseh Desoto explaining his "Understanding Poverty" exhibit on the *Learning for Justice* site. He states, "When you don't have the money to shelter yourself or to even buy a meal for yourself your world narrows down. A world that you're not participating in because you can't compete" (2009). Students might also examine the supports that exist, such as an "EBT card" (p. 98) to which Zoey refers in the novel, which allowed her mom to fill the fridge with the coffee yogurt she loves.

The yogurt that makes Zoey so happy refers to an aspect of the novel it is crucial not to overlook while reading. Despite her situation, Zoey has close ties with her family. When she waits on the bus for her siblings, she states, "I'm always right there, waiting for them. Always. Maybe we don't have dinner at a table every night. Maybe they have to get free lunch tickets and deal with all the same shame I had to deal with when I was first in school. But at the end of the day, I'm always there to pick them up" (p. 49). She cares deeply about her brother and sister and is the only one who seems to be able to calm Bryce down when he has tantrums and needs comfort. In another moment in the text, Zoey expresses joy in watching football at Lenny's house: "Both of us are always on the edge of the couch for every third down, me eating those cheese puffs and him drinking his soda. Basically, it's the best time ever" (p. 10). While taking care not to romanticize these moments, teachers can highlight how Zoey finds joy and connection as she is able to. They can emphasize that people are not just the trauma that they have experienced. While living with limited income is a big part of Zoey's daily life, there is more to her life than just that. Students might illustrate one of these scenes and use quotes to support their renderings.

After Reading

Upon completing the novel, students can reflect on how the story depicts the cycle of poverty and the factors that perpetuate it. For example, Zoey's mom experiences a lack of health care that contributed to her situation with Lenny. Zoey remembers: "that was when she had to keep a bag of frozen corn on her face to numb the pain from her rotting teeth—because some people have parents who remind them to brush their teeth, but my mom didn't . . . She finally had to sell our beat up car to scrape together the money to get those teeth extracted" (p. 24). Without a car, her life became more difficult. She has to walk to work, which takes time and physical energy. Then she met Lenny, who paid for her dental work, but that created her feelings of indebtedness to him seen in the novel. Zoey also knew, "my mom's lucky to have this job. It's not as much money as the fancy place she worked in the tiny little mountain town of Peru, Vermont, where all the skiers came, but you can't keep a job like that if your car doesn't start when it's cold out" (p. 43). Students could create flow charts from the novel to show how these factors compounded and affected their financial situation, noting how they piled upon one another. Zoey asks: "How is it possible to have no visible cage around you, but to be so trapped?" (p. 108). Teachers might ask: *What is the cage to which Zoey refers? What other situations might make people feel trapped like she does?*

The title of the novel refers to a metaphor Zoey uses throughout the novel as her way to escape an uncomfortable situation. The octopus is her favorite animal largely because of its ability to do many things at once with its arms. She says, "If I were an octopus, things would be so much easier. I'd have one arm to wipe Aurora's nose. Two more for holding both kids' hands when I pick them up from the Head Start bus stop . . . One to adjust my shirt because it doesn't really fit and it can get too revealing if I'm not paying attention, and I don't want to be 'that girl'" (p. 4–5). Teachers could first task students with drawing an octopus and what it represents to Zoey with specific references to the text. Then they could choose their own animal as a metaphor for what they wish they could do in their own lives and create an artistic rendering accompanied by an artist's statement that explains their choice. They might display these in the classroom or in a public space in the school.

Students could also research the long-term effects of poverty. As mentioned in the pre reading TedX talk, trauma from living in poverty can last well after a person is financially secure. Zoey describes a night when she was four: "My mom and I had been sleeping in our car for weeks, and I woke up to see a man's face at the window, trying to break in to steal all our stuff and maybe more. You might think that would mean lockdowns don't scare me as much. But they only scare me more" (p. 128). Readers could match their findings with Zoey's experiences and suggest mechanisms for addressing them (for more on teaching about trauma, see Chapter 1).

Finally, students will likely wonder why it took Kara "so long," or "so many reasons" to leave Lenny. This is a common narrative in public discourse about people living in poverty and living with abuse, which are concurrent in this text. Teachers could ask students to create responses to these questions from the text, using quotes and examples. When Zoey's mom does visit Family Services, for instance, she learns there is "Not a single opening for low-income housing . . . The waiting list is years long" (p. 207). This is indicative of why people are unhoused or stay in negative situations, as Zoey's mom does. Initially also, she tells Zoey that Lenny deserves a second chance, stating: "Instead of automatically giving up and going back to the broken toilet apartment? Instead of giving up on my kids having a father figure? Instead of giving up on having a boyfriend who can hold a job and tells me that my cooking smells good?" (p. 200). Her words here explain her desire to provide stability for her children and to hold onto the home they have. Students could therefore draw upon these instances to craft retorts, similar to the debates in the text, as to why and how poverty limits Kara's options.

INTERSECTIONS

As mentioned above, the most dominant intersection with social class in the book is domestic abuse. Zoey notes again and again how her mom changed after she met Lenny, how "She used to tell great jokes" (p. 9) and be more confident. Lenny's treatment, however, demeans her mother and greatly affects her self-esteem. In one scene when he makes her cry after chastising her for buying yogurt instead of meat, he responds: "Oh poor baby . . . Turn on the waterworks to see if that'll help. But sorry, you're not going to manipulate me that way" (p. 105). He tells her, "If you didn't have me to take care of you, you'd be out on the street. And no one cares about a chick on the street" (p. 105) therefore denigrating her and making her feel as if he is her only option. He even says, "You're such a joke" (p. 106) and blames her when he loses his job even though he was the one who lost his temper with a client and was fired. Teachers could ask students how Lenny exhibits abusive behavior, though without physical harm, and emphasize that his words nonetheless denote verbal assault and abuse. This point is reflected in the text, as Kara tells Zoey when she considers calling the domestic violence hotline, "I don't know. Do you think I should? He's never hit me" (p. 209) to which Zoey responds, "Mom. You're scared. I'm scared. That counts" (p. 209). This exchange is crucial and shows young readers that emotional abuse, verbal comments, and threats of physical violence warrant action. Defining these aspects would be beneficial for readers who may not be aware of these lines.

Foster care is also an intersection in the book. Fuschia, Zoey's best friend, lives in a similarly limited housing situation with her mother. Fuschia, however, has been in foster care before due to her mother's drug addiction, and she battles ideas of returning if she calls DCF (Department of Child and Family) at the idea of having to move in with her mother's boyfriend, who shoots a gun in the car with Fushcia after school one day to scare her. Students could research the information regarding foster care and myths connected to visits from Child Protective Services and foster care (see Chapter 9 on teaching about foster care). Teachers could ask: *Why does Fuschia debate calling for help? Why does she feel like she doesn't have real choices in the matter? Why doesn't she tell anyone about the scene in the car with the gun?*

Finally, bullying is a large part of the book. As described earlier, Zoey is bullied for her clothing and supposed smell on the bus. Another character, Silas, who is Zoey's neighbor, is similarly bullied but has built a wall around himself to protect himself from his peer's insults. This wall is penetrated, however, when he is accused of shooting the gun in the parking lot after school, and he is tormented at school as the suspected shooter. Zoey says, "I heard a couple of girls started crying and refused to be in the same room as Silas during English class" (p. 140). When Zoey tells Silas she knows he wasn't the shooter, she sees "a tear escaping from one of his squeezed shut eyes" (p. 180). Teachers could focus readers' attention on the effects of bullying on Silas's mental health and have them design scenarios that could have occurred in the book to alleviate the bullying (for teaching about bullying, see Chapter 3).

IDEAS FOR SOCIAL ACTION

Given the multiple topics this book addresses, students could extend their discussions and activities into social action projects readily. First, they could use the T-charts about the ways schools lack resources (from the During Reading strategies) and select one for which to advocate to school officials, such as an art supply room with poster board and other materials necessary to create class projects. Leaving it up to the teacher to offer and the student to ask can increase stigma, but having a dedicated space that students can visit on their own and take what they need creates a more welcoming environment. Aligned with this, students could envision and act on ways to address the belonging aspect that is emphasized in the TEDx Talk from the Pre-Reading strategies. They might design inclusion campaigns and share messages on social media or encourage peers to invite individuals outside of their immediate friend groups to join during lunch, in class group work, or during after school activities. These campaigns could also include issues around bullying, as readers saw frequently with regard to both Zoey and Silas. Helping each other pay attention to who is and is not included and making a concerted effort can increase action and empathy.

From their research on minimum wage, students could select an employer or local official to contact about steps that must be taken to raise their own state's or even another state's minimum wage, depending on their context. Students could create infographics with data from their learning about poverty thresholds and costs of living to serve as evidence for their arguments. They could use Zoey's experience as a narrative example of how issues compound that affect work, health care, and safety and could retell her story or another from their previous research to solicit understanding and compassion. They can identify employers in their communities that offer a livable wage with needed benefits as well as places of employment that are accessible via public transportation or safe walkways.

In the book, Connor is Zoey's mother's co-worker who helps watch the baby and offers his car when they decide to leave Lenny. Students could use Connor's position to motivate others to assist people in need in ways that are meaningful and supportive. They could draw on the resources that Zoey needed to partner with a local shelter or food bank and collect for those similarly in need. They can identify places that offer free or affordable childcare (for both healthy and sick children) and share this information in public places like shelters, the grocery, or the library. They could designate collection spots at school or by classroom and advertise their efforts so that their peers could contribute. They could collect not only food and clothing but also other items that could help facilitate that sense of belonging mentioned previously, such as games, sunglasses, or jewelry, that might go beyond initial basic needs.

Finally, to address the issue of abuse in the novel and particularly verbal abuse, students might partner with their school counselor and any related organization in the community to host a guest speaker panel that explains signs and resources related to domestic violence. Not only did Lenny make Kara think she was always at fault, but readers also learn he intentionally isolated her from her friendship with Fuschia's mom. A speaker on these topics would need to be age-appropriate and at the teacher's discretion, but Zoey's experience is not uncommon, and teaching youth to recognize these issues can give them the tools they need to help themselves and others. Especially when many (as did Kara) worry that abuse is only constituted by physical force, it is important to also shed light on the manifestations and consequences of other forms. If they opened the event to the public, students could collect donations at the door and offer free childcare, and then they could donate the proceeds to a shelter or other organization that supports families escaping domestic violence.

As a whole then, *The Benefits of Being an Octopus* (Braden, 2018) provides students with opportunities to better understand systemic poverty and social class disparities in the United States. An awareness of the prevalence of poverty as well as other social justice issues that overlap with and/or can be exacerbated by having limited income and resources can help students to identify barriers as well as ways to address the effects of this system of oppression.

SUPPLEMENTAL RESOURCES

Connected Young Adult Literature

The Remarkable Journey of Coyote Sunrise by Dan Gemeinhart
Rural Voices: 15 Authors Challenge Assumptions about Small Town America by Nora Carpenter (Editor)
Look Both Ways: A Tale Told in Ten Blocks by Jason Reynolds
Amal Unbound by Aisha Saeed
Counting by Sevens by Holly Sloan

Connected Music

"I Need a Dollar" by Aloe Blacc
"I'm Busted" by Johnny Cash
"Nobody Knows When You're Down and Out" by Eric Clapton
"Fortunate Son" by Creedence Clearwater Revival

"Dear Landlord" by Bob Dylan
"Dead End Street" by the Kinks
"Mr. Banker" by Lynyrd Skynyrd

Connected Poetry

The Borgen Project. 4 Poems about Poverty. https://borgenproject.org/4-poems-about-poverty/
"Your Riches—taught me—poverty" by Emily Dickinson
"Poem of a Few Greatnesses" by Walt Whitman

REFERENCES

Braden, A. (2018). *The benefits of being an octopus.* Sky Pony Press.
Desoto, B. T. (2009). Understanding poverty exhibit. *Learning for Justice.* https://www.learningforjustice.org/classroom-resources/texts/ben-desoto-understanding-poverty-exhibit
Kochhar, R. & Sechopoulos, S. (2022). How the American middle class has changed in the past five decades. *Pew Research Center.* https://www.pewresearch.org/fact-tank/2022/04/20/how-the-american-middle-class-has-changed-in-the-past-five-decades/
Learning for Justice. (2022). Issues of poverty. *Southern Poverty Law Center.* https://www.learningforjustice.org/classroom-resources/lessons/issues-of-poverty
Lino, M. (2020). The cost of raising a child. *U.S. Department of Agriculture.* https://www.usda.gov/media/blog/2017/01/13/cost-raising-child
Matteo, M. (2022). How this entrepreneur is working to help Black women build generational wealth through home ownership. CNBC.com. https://www.cnbc.com/select/what-is-generational-wealth/
Miale, K. (2016). Moving beyond basic needs to break the cycle of poverty. TEDxTalks. https://www.youtube.com/watch?v=F8SbHzW-8Es
State Minimum Wage Laws. (2022). *U.S. Department of Labor.* https://www.dol.gov/agencies/whd/minimum-wage/state
Waddell, B. (2021). Report: $15 hourly wage isn't livable anywhere in the U.S. *U.S. News & World Report.* https://www.usnews.com/news/best-states/articles/2021-08-06/report-15-hourly-wage-isnt-livable-anywhere-in-the-us

Chapter 3

Bullying

Though not a new topic, bullying remains at the forefront of discussions in K-12 schools and especially in the middle schools. Stakeholders, parents, and educators today more fully understand the dire consequences of bullying than in the past. As a result, schools have developed more cohesive definitions and responses. Efforts to teach young people about bullying and attempts to thwart it are therefore, typically, well underway.

It is important for teachers to understand what constitutes bullying not only to recognize it when it occurs but also to feel confident leading effective related instruction. Instead of merely "being mean," bullying involves consistent and targeted negative behavior. The American Psychological Association (APA), for example, defines bullying as "aggressive behavior that is intentional and involves an imbalance of power or strength. It is a repeated behavior and can be physical, verbal, or relational" (APA, 2011, para 1). The APA provides advice for teachers and school administrators regarding bullying, encouraging them to "be knowledgeable and observant" (para 3), to "involve students and parents" (para 4), and to "set positive expectations about behavior for students and adults" (para 5). They also suggest preventative measures such as having "anti-bullying documents" (para 5) that students and parents/guardians sign as well as developing strategies with children for how to respond if they are ever bullied.

Ryan and Hurst (2021) encourage a more nuanced view of bullying, noting that the bully-victim dyad is often the only presentation young people receive of bullying, when in reality bullying "is situated within complex social systems which have become established and reproduced over time" (p. 418). Along these lines, it is therefore crucial to note that many socially marginalized groups are intentionally targeted for bullying and to recognize how such violent behavior reflects trends and broader narratives. For instance, in 2019 the Centers for Disease Control and Prevention (CDC) released the national Youth Risk Behavior Surveillance results, which showed that 43% of transgender youth have been bullied on school property (Roberts, 2020, para 2). Students with disabilities or students whose religious observances are different from the majority at their school may also become recipients of bullying. As a social justice issue, therefore, bullying intersects with other areas of oppression including race, class, gender, and sexuality, and it needs to be studied along these lines. When discussing bullying with young people, unpacking these systems and broader narratives should accompany the conversation.

Examining such broader contexts illustrates that bullying expands beyond small scale one-on-one or group-on-one interactions. Rather, bullying is impacted by and reflected in the media, through politicians, actors, and socialites. These entities can encourage *or* hinder bullying. For instance, following President Trump's tweet referring to COVID-19 as the "Chinese Virus," the United States experienced an increase in harassment of Asian Americans (Kurtzman, 2021). In March of 2022, Instagram suspended Kanye West for his harassment of Pete Davidson, his ex-wife Kim Kardashian's then new boyfriend, which also resulted in West's fans bullying Davidson. These are simply two instances among multiple instances of bullying which occur on a daily basis and which our students see all around them.

As these examples show, while bullying can and often does take place in school buildings, in more recent years, cyberbullying has been on the rise. This insidious form "includes sending, posting, or sharing negative, harmful, false, or mean content about someone else. It can include sharing personal or private information about someone else causing embarrassment or humiliation." In the age of cellphones and text messages and through TikTok, Instagram, Snapchat, and other media venues, youth can spread messages quickly and even anonymously, creating a situation difficult to stop once it begins. This is evident in the story of Hope Witsell, a thirteen year old from Florida whose nude photo, intended for her boyfriend, was shared by another student with students across six schools. She experienced massive online bullying as a result, with the creation of a "Hope Hater Page," and she ultimately died by suicide (Kaye, 2010).

The story of Hope illustrates one outcome, but the effects of bullying are wide ranging. A number of suicides and school shootings have been linked to bullying. In fact, stopbullying.gov (2021) reported that "in twelve of fifteen school-shooting cases in the 1990s, the shooters had a history of being bullied," (para 6), illustrating the far-reaching ramifications such actions can incur. On an individual scale, bullying can lead to depression and anxiety, decreased academic achievement, and health deterioration.

Social media can, however, also be used as an instrument to stop bullying, and this is an important point to note. There are a number of websites and campaigns dedicated to addressing bullying. For example, Stomp Out Bullying (2021) has a "See Me" campaign that encourages individuals to use the hashtag #SeeMe and instructs them on making videos that express what others should see when they look at the person, not perhaps what they might initially see, such as skin color or a disability. Instagram (2019) instituted a "restrict" function, which it says is "designed to empower you to quietly protect your account while still keeping an eye on a bully" (para 1). The feature, when enabled, makes a comment visible only to that person. These examples illustrate that the web is also a place where we can work against bullying.

Given these contexts, it is crucial that we, as teachers and as a society, continue to work with students around defining, recognizing, and disrupting bullying. Often overlooked or downplayed by adults, bullying deserves critical and serious attention and should not be taken lightly. As such, in this chapter we offer the novel *Genesis Begins Again* (Williams, 2020) as an example of the bullying linked to racism and as a demonstration of its impact on the recipient's self-image.

GENESIS BEGINS AGAIN

In *Genesis Begins Again* (2020), Alicia D. Williams tells the poignant story of a thirteen year old girl, Genesis, and her struggle with her identity, family, and friends. Born to a light-skinned Black mother and a dark-skinned Black father, Genesis constantly battles her self-image, wishing she were a lighter complexion. As her father abuses alcohol and her family experiences eviction, she moves to a new school. Having been bullied by a group of girls at her former school, she meets Sophia and Troy who become her genuine friends. Throughout the novel, Genesis learns of the history of colorism in her own family from her grandmother, who explains the "paper bag test," in which her own father wished for his children to find spouses whose skin was lighter than the brown color of a paper bag because he found this correlated to social advancement (p. 151).

Genesis slowly finds her voice as the story unfolds, and she comes to accept herself with the support of her music teacher, Mrs. Hill, who introduces her to Black women singers to whom Genesis relates. Troy, whose parents encourage his reading of W. E. B. Du Bois and Malcolm X so that he knows he "can still be great" (p. 99) also provides Genesis with a lens of pride, and Sophia, who struggles with obsessive compulsive disorder (OCD) helps Genesis reject other people's opinions and be more confident in who she is. In the end, Genesis gains a deeper understanding of what fuels her father's alcoholism and resolves to value herself more.

TEACHING STRATEGIES

Before Reading

Prior to reading *Genesis,* students will need to develop a shared understanding of bullying. Teachers can start by having students brainstorm in small groups on posters or white boards definitions and examples of bullying. They can direct students to think of both in-school and out-of-school examples so as to open space for a discussion of cyberbullying and bullying that is done outside of school.

Students might then complete a survey that asks them questions such as: *Who is often the most targeted for bullying in school (those of a certain gender identity, ethnicity, sexuality, etc.)? What factors might cause someone to be a bully? What are the effects of bullying on both the person committing the bullying and the person being bullied? What is the policy related to bullying in our school?*

Once students have attempted to answer these questions, they can then conduct research to check and correct (if needed) their responses, consulting sites such as stopbullying.gov and the Centers for Disease Control's Youth Risk Behavior Surveillance System information. They can note what they knew, what they did not, and why those discrepancies might exist.

With a partner, students might research examples of bullying covered in the media and report to the class. These could include Isabella Tichenor, Eli Fritchley, and Jamari Dent, for example. Then, the whole class could compare contributing factors, effects, and outcomes across the cases, noting how each bullying story shares commonalities. They could then return to their definitions of bullying and add to their objective descriptions. Teachers should use discretion on which cases students research, as some may be triggering for their students. However—as we noted in the introduction and throughout this text—since this is a real issue that students face daily, we encourage educators to treat bullying as a serious social topic and to honor the victims and their stories.

In addition to cultivating an understanding of bullying, teachers should also ensure that students are familiar with the notion of colorism, as this is a pervasive theme in the book. Knight (2015) explains it as "Within-group and between-group prejudice in favor of lighter skin color" (para. 2). The history of colorism, how it manifests, and perhaps most importantly, why it exists and persists are crucial to unpack. Helping students in understanding that colorism is connected to internalized, institutionalized racism so as not to mistake it as within-group racism is especially paramount.

To help students apply colorism to modern contexts, students might watch the video "Confessions of a D Girl: Colorism and Global Standards of

Beauty," in which Stanford graduate student Chika Okoro (2016) recounts her experience with casting calls for films and shares how not even Beyoncé would make "the cut" for the movie she describes. Students could then extend their understanding and find contemporary examples in television, film, advertising, and music of where colorism prevails.

Teachers could also introduce students to controversies associated with Dove, the skincare company, and the backlash they have received for advertisements that reinforce the equation of whiteness with beauty. CBS News (2016) covered one story in which Dove was criticized for a commercial in which a dark skinned woman pulls her shirt off to expose a lighter skinned woman underneath who is presumably "clean."

In the novel, colorism is directly connected to Genesis's bullying and resulting negative self-image. Therefore, it will be crucial for students to discern how messages such as those in the Dove commercial are relayed in society. When investigating this or other advertisements, teachers could ask: *What is the message of this* [Dove] *advertisement? How could this be interpreted differently by audiences of different races? Why is it important to think critically about media?*

During Reading

As students read, they can keep a log of instances when Genesis experiences bullying and note how those relate to their definitions prior to reading. From the outset, Genesis shares "The List," which two girls made in the fifth grade and which shares *One Hundred Reasons Why We Hate Genesis* (Williams, 2020, p. 6). Genesis adds her own reasons to the list throughout the novel. This in itself is an instance of bullying with clearly harmful psychological effects on Genesis. As they read, students can track how these and other instances of bullying by other classmates directly affect Genesis, keeping a running cause-and-effect quote journal.

The bullying examples in this novel involve power, repeated action, and connections to broader social groupings that would be important to dissect in order for students to fully delve into bullying. Youth might also relate these to the factual examples they researched, comparing and contrasting the types of bullying (verbal, physical, etc.) and their effects on the recipient. This can help students see that Genesis is one example amongst a host of types of bullying and help detract from the single narrative of bullying.

Drawing on the work of Ryan and Hurst (2021), teachers might also facilitate students' discernment of the complexity of bullying by expanding the victim-bully dyad to talk more about bystanders and contexts. For instance, when Genesis first gets to her new school, one student facetiously comments, "Cute outfit," and then adds "Where'd you get it, Goodwill?" (Williams,

2020, p. 54) to which everyone laughs. Another student refers to her skin color as "burnt" (p. 56) and later, a student calls her the school's "first international student! . . . All the way from Africa!" (p. 105). In these scenarios, which involve repeated verbal insults, there were multiple other students present who could have intervened. Emphasizing those students' role complexifies bullying and tasks students with thinking more about complicity. It is easy for youth to think of bullying in only simplistic terms, but by the time they get to middle school their cognitive capacities are ready to see the surrounding social milieu and how that plays into such issues.

In addition, Genesis is not the only character in the novel who is bullied. Troy is harassed at school by a group of boys who expect him to provide his notes to them and help with their schoolwork, and those students call him "Bill Nye" (p. 62), even after Troy has asked them not to. They continue to pester Troy later in the novel, blaming him for their bad grades. In discussing these other instances of bullying with readers, teachers could ask: *Who else was nearby when these comments were made to the character? What are those individuals' roles in bullying? What could they have done to disrupt the situation?* This can help students begin to think through the actual bullying situation and again remove the bully-victim dyad. Students can determine action/steps for the characters and for others involved that would help alleviate the situations.

As Genesis and Sophia develop a friendship, Genesis learns that Sophia has OCD and has experienced related bullying. Sophia tells Genesis "it makes me nervous when people touch my stuff" (p. 233), and she is very particular about silverware placement at her home before dinner. Genesis begins to realize that Sophia is not friends with the "popular" girls but seems to have been at one time, and Sophia shares that after she confided in one of the girls in the popular group, that same girl "made up a cartoon called 'Fear the Walking Freak'" (p. 320) in which Sophia was the main character. This sort of harassment surrounds mental health, another aspect important for noting with student readers. A teacher, therefore, could have students consider why and how Sophia is being bullied. Students could research OCD and discern how Sophia's symptoms match what they find (and how they do not). Students can note times they have heard of OCD and in what ways and consider how Sophia upholds and disrupts these.

Youth readers could also research what sorts of protections exist against bullying, especially as related to race or mental health, and what sorts of related legislation exists. For example, while there is no federal legislation against bullying, schools are obligated to respond, if harassment is related to other forms of negative behavior including the use of derogatory language and the creation of a hostile environment (stopbullying.gov, 2021).

Students can also return to their previous brainstorming around bullying and revisit the groups they labeled who experience it, noting if they included those who experience neurodivergence like Sophia or those who have darker skin like Genesis. They can again use this to discuss how bullying can occur around issues of social oppression. To think about these topics and to delve further into the text, teachers could ask: *What history did Genesis learn from her grandmother related to color (race) and society? How is this still affecting her own place in her world? Why might students bully Sophia, despite knowing that she has a medical diagnosis? What examples of similar types of bullying (e.g., related to disabilities) have you seen in your own lives and in the media?*

After Reading

As a reflection on the whole novel, readers could create flow charts of the development of Genesis's self-esteem. This could be based from the cause/effect charts mentioned in the previous section, but be expanded by having students then note ways Genesis's self-esteem was enhanced or how she made efforts to change it. Genesis starts out feeling very low about herself and struggles throughout the novel but through Mrs. Hill's introduction to music, Troy's pride in his culture, and Sophia's friendship, she gains confidence in herself. Labeling each of these entities can help youth perceive outlets for themselves as well as avenues for support.

Along those lines, students can journal about what helps them with their own self-esteem, be that an adult, like Genesis's music teacher, or a creative space, such as art. They can construct their own self-esteem poem or mantra that they can draw upon if they are ever feeling doubts about themselves. In addition, for Troy, reading about his heritage and noting accomplishments of famous Black men helped him remain confident despite being taunted by his peers. Students might explore individuals who inspire them and generate projects around those, composing short research papers accompanied by flyers about that person. They could even research famous people who have experienced bullying and been vocal about their stories, such as Demi Levato, Shawn Mendes, or Tom Ford.

After finishing the novel, students might also extend their thinking about bullying and context by discussing the similarities and differences between the schools that Genesis attended and especially the environment at Farmington Hills. Teachers might ask: *How are "new kids" often received in schools? How could bullying vary depending on the demographics at a school? What motivates people to bully, and why do you think those in the novel were bullies?*

In another after-reading activity, students could revisit the cover of the book and discuss how it reflects the major themes of the novel, especially bullying. They might design a new cover that they feel captures the elements they found most compelling and share those with their classmates. Finally, students could watch the video of the author, Alicia D. Williams (2022), responding to a student question and in which she discussed her own experiences with bullying. After watching, students could make a list of questions they might still want to ask the author, and perhaps the teacher could send those to the author via email or social media platforms.

INTERSECTIONS

As mentioned above, the book has a number of intersections with other systems of oppression. In particular, Genesis's struggle with colorism adds to her lack of self-esteem. Her father tells her in a drunken state one night, "You were supposed to come out looking like her! . . . Look at you with your black" (p. 112) and then her mother cuts him off. Genesis internalizes this to mean that her father wishes she did not inherit his skin color but rather her mother's. This painful memory is a significant cause of Genesis's lack of self-esteem and her desire to be lighter skinned, which she attempts to accomplish through extreme measures. In one instance, she exfoliates her skin and then squeezes lemon juice onto it, which is painful. She even goes so far as to secretly use her mother's credit card to purchase skin lightening cream, applying it to her body which damages her skin and causes light spots on her face. She says, at one point, "see my hands. My black hands. My feet. My black feet. Black and dirty. Filthy. I hate it!" (p. 197).

Her friends at school notice, but she concocts a story to cover the outcome, which is her splotchy skin. Students could select a character from the book or from another book, television show, or movie that deals with self-image and draw pictures of the way that character might look to their friends versus how they see themselves. They could post these in the room and complete a gallery walk, noting patterns amongst them. The teacher could then lead students through a conversation of what discrepancies exist between the two images and what commonalities the drawings had with classmates'. This could also lead to a dialogue in which students share about themselves in the same way if they are comfortable doing so.

Another prominent intersection in this book related to the situation above is that of substance abuse. Genesis's father struggles with alcohol, causing him to lose his job and incur repeated evictions from homes. By the end of the novel, Genesis has learned that her father experienced a tough childhood, having lost his brother, Charlie, and dealt with his mother's accompanying grief.

He tells Genesis how his own mother told him "over and over she wished it was me dead, steada Charlie" (p. 355), which clearly deeply affected him. He tells Genesis: "me saying those words to you . . . were because . . . I didn't want you to be nothin' like me—not act like me, look like me" (p. 355), explaining the comment that so profoundly hurt her. He obviously struggled with his own self-esteem and did not wish that for his daughter. He also attends Genesis's talent show at the end of the novel and expresses his pride in his daughter's performance. After reading, students could dissect and discuss the father's character. Teachers could ask: *How can we better understand Genesis's father's actions and words given what we learned about his background? How do you understand Genesis's mother's love for her father—why does she stay with/go back to him? What should her father do differently to communicate with Genesis and show her that he loves her?*

This is a delicate intersection and should be treated as such; teachers will want to ensure not to justify Genesis's father's abuse and his negative treatment of her. However, the situation provides a powerful opportunity to look at the complexity of people and how sometimes we can love a person without loving their actions–we can love a person while being cognizant of their addictions and behaviors. In these discussions, teachers' guidance is also necessary not to shame the mother for staying with the father and/or returning to him, as again, they live in a complicated situation that is reflective of real life relationships. To better explore this topic, readers could research strategies for family members coping with the addiction of a loved one.

Finally, poverty is another system of oppression in the novel that intersects with bullying and substance abuse. In the opening chapter of the novel, Genesis's family is evicted, which she learns when she brings several "friends" home after school to find her family's belongings in the yard. To note this intersection, teachers could ask: *How does the bullying Genesis experiences relate to her family's financial status? Why is it so important to Genesis and her mother to stay in their new house in Farmington Hills? What challenges does Genesis's mother face in wanting to return to school?* For other ideas related to teaching about poverty, see Chapter 2.

IDEAS FOR SOCIAL ACTION

Given these numerous intersections, there are a plethora of avenues for students to take regarding social action projects. Over the years, state legislation has begun to address bullying, yet there is still progress to be made. Students might first research the local policies for bullying in their school and/or district and determine if these are stringent and encompassing. If not, they could provide research-based recommendations and present them to the appropriate officials (e.g., principal, counselor). At the state level, they could write letters to legislators on policies they would like to see in place and even create a video to share widely calling for actions they feel are needed. This video could be disseminated widely to solicit support and more attention from lawmakers.

In thinking specifically about bullying and intersections, students could create informational campaigns related to colorism and share them in their school, creating posters or flyers to distribute. This could also be done in relation to bullying and mental health. Youth might establish a list of common ways they see bullying—through certain words or small actions—and then generate ways to disrupt these when they occur. For instance, in the novel, Sophia shares, "I don't have friends because I got tired of their teasing, especially behind my back. Weirdo, Freak, you name it, they called me it" (p. 237). Providing tangible, disruptive phrases and actions for students when they overhear words like these can help students imagine how to actually move from bystander to protestor. They might write and perform skits in which they envision carrying out such interactions so they can feel and show what taking a stand against bullying will look like. The skits could be recorded and shared on the school's newscast if one exists or simply shared in classrooms or on a school webpage. Because sometimes students lose track of the seriousness of the issue in their enjoyment of performing, it will be important for teachers to oversee the process, ensuring that the skits/videos are accurate and provide authentic scenarios and methods for disruption.

Students could also design projects that resist common uses and misunderstandings of bullying, racism, and OCD. These might include designing slogans around the fact that proper terms are important, which could serve to counter misuses of the words as seen in the novel (e.g., "It's not OCD, you just like to be neat. Language matters."). They could also note what *is* and *is not* bullying (e.g., "If I ask you not to make fun of something and you continue to, that's bullying," or "Saying, 'I'm not racist, BUT' actually isn't ok"). These sorts of visual media explicitly address harmful language and the perpetuation of problematic ideologies. They would be beneficial to set the tone in a school or classroom and to plant seeds of change within students' discourse.

Youth are aware of the types of bullying that go on in their schools and, as such, can address targeted actions for it. For example, in one study (Boyd & Miller, 2020), students in an affluent school recognized that their peers were bullied for not wearing brand name clothing and led a movement to remind folks in their school that they are a person and not a brand. In another example (Kist, Srsen, & Bishop, 2015), students at Bay High took to Twitter to combat negative tweets about their classmates with a flood of affirming messages about those same individuals. Bullying around students with special needs and based on sexuality is also prevalent in many schools, and as such students could design related campaigns. This again helps reinforce that social action projects are based on problems that students discern and that they determine are dire.

In terms of self-esteem, social action projects may start with individuals as they identify ways in which they can be kinder and more supportive to others and span to social media and school-wide events aimed at encouraging and celebrating the uniqueness that all have to offer. For instance, having students put sticky notes with positive affirmations on a designated space in the school, or sharing them with classmates could boost morale. This activity could be extended to places where people may need a confidence boost such as outside of the counselor's office, at a local hospital, or at a nursing home. A "pay it forward" day could encourage students to do something nice for someone else based on something that has been done for them in the past. This could open conversations about empathy and respect.

As a whole, *Genesis Begins Again* (Williams, 2020) offers readers and teachers vast possibilities for thinking and acting critically around bullying and its intersections with other systems of oppression. Through reading, discussing, reflecting, and engaging, students can become more understanding of their fellow classmates and more critical of their worlds.

SUPPLEMENTAL RESOURCES

Connected Websites and Lessons

"Bullying in the News," National Association of People Against Bullying https://www.napab.org/bullying-in-the-news.

"The Hidden Harms of Racial Bullying" by Deidre McPhillips; US News World Report https://www.usnews.com/news/healthiest-communities/articles/2019-05-23/bullying-victims-more-likely-to-use-drugs-alcohol-analysis-shows

Stop Bullying: https://www.stopbullying.gov/

Learning for Justice: Bullying Basics https://www.learningforjustice.org/professional development/bullying-basics

Resources to Fight Bullying and Harassment at School: https://www.edutopia.org/article/bullying-prevention-resources

Connected Young Adult Literature

Wonder by R. J. Palacio
Fish in a Tree by Lynda Mullaly Hunt
Restart by Gordan Korman
Booked by Kwame Alexander

The Great Wall of Lucy Wu by Wendy Wan-Long Shang
Bullied: A Modern Day Look at Middle School Bullying by Scott Langteau and Erik Ly (Illustrator)
Starfish by Lisa Fipps

Connected Movies

A Girl Like Her, Netflix
The Fat Boy Chronicles
Cyberbully, ABC Family

Connected Music

"Mean" by Taylor Swift
"Who Says" by Selena Gomez
"Dem Haters" by Rihanna
"Hate on Me" by Jill Scott

REFERENCES

American Psychological Association. (2011). How parents, teachers, and kids can take action to prevent bullying. https://www.apa.org/topics/bullying/prevent.

Boyd, A. & Miller, J. (2020). Let's give them something to talk (and act!) about: Privilege, racism, and oppression in the middle school classroom. *Voices from the Middle, 27*(3), 15–19.

CBS News. (2017, October 9). Dove apologizes for racially insensitive ad. https://www.cbsnews.com/news/dove-ad-racist-insensitive-apology-for-facebook-ad/

Instagram. (2019, October 2). Introducing the 'restrict' feature to protect against bullying. https://about.instagram.com/blog/announcements/stand-up-against-bullying-with-restrict

Kaye, R. (2010, October 7). How a cell phone picture led to a girl's suicide. http://www.cnn.com/2010/LIVING/10/07/hope.witsells.story/index.html.

Kist, W., Srsen, K., & Bishop, B. F. (2015). Social media and 'kids today': A counter-narrative from a US high school. *English Journal, 104*(3), 41–46.

Knight, D. (2015). What's "colorism"?: How would your students answer this question? *Learning for Justice, 51.* https://www.learningforjustice.org/magazine/fall-2015/whats-colorism.

Kurtzman, L. (2021, March 18). Trump's 'Chinese Virus' tweet linked to rise of Anti-Asian hashtags on Twitter. https://www.ucsf.edu/news/2021/03/420081/trumps-chinese-virus-tweet-linked-rise-anti-asian-hashtags-twitter.

Okoro, C. (2016). Confessions of a D girl: Colorism and global standards of beauty. TEDxStanford. https://www.youtube.com/watch?v=fvoWoMIwr-g

Roberts, M. (2020, August 26). New CDC data shows LGBTQ youth are more likely to be bullied than straight cisgender youth. https://www.hrc.org/news/new-cdc-data-shows-lgbtq-youth-are-more-likely-to-be-bullied-than-straight-cisgender-youth).

Ryan, E. & Hurst, H. (2021). Bullying always seemed less complicated before I read: Developing adolescents' understandings of the complex social architecture of bullying through a YAL book club. *Research in the Teaching of English, 55*(4), 416–440.

Stomp Out Bullying. (2021). Stomp out bullying: End the hate . . . change the culture. #SeeMe campaign. https://www.stompoutbullying.org/see-me-campaign

stopbullying.gov. (2021, May 21). Effects of bullying. https://www.stopbullying.gov/bullying/effects

Williams, A. D. (2020). *Genesis begins again.* Atheneum Books for Young Readers.

Williams, A. D. (2022, February 1). Q&A with author Alicia D. Williams: What was your inspiration for Genesis Begins Again? https://www.youtube.com/watch?v=1kbqFKxL0Eg.

Chapter 4

Refugee Crisis

The number of refugees across the globe is at an all-time high, having "crossed the milestone of one-hundred million for the first time on record, propelled by the war in Ukraine and other conflicts" (Siegfried, 2022). A refugee is "someone who is unable or unwilling to return to their country of origin owing to a well-founded fear of being persecuted for reasons of race, religion, nationality, membership of a particular social group, or political opinion" (UNHCR, 2001–2021), and someone with refugee status has a right to international protection (Amnesty International, 2022).

An asylum-seeker, like a refugee, has "left their country and is seeking protection from persecution and serious human-rights violations in another country, but who hasn't yet been legally recognized as a refugee and is waiting to receive a decision on their asylum claim. While every country has their own specific guidelines for applying for refugee status, typically it includes needing a referral from an embassy or especially trained NGO, as well as extensive security screening, interviews, and medical examinations. Seeking asylum is a human right. This means everyone should be allowed to enter another country to seek asylum" (Amnesty International. 2022, para 11).

In contrast, the term "migrant" has no legal definition. A migrant is someone who has left their home country. It can be for a multitude of reasons, including opportunities for education, jobs, or to be with family. While it is possible and often the case that migrants also are in danger in their home country, if they have not applied for refugee status, they do not have legal rights to protection.

What makes refugee status unique is that there are legal protections in place. An individual must have applied for and been granted asylum in a country before they can apply for refugee status. All of this is time consuming, and as such, it is even more alarming that so many individuals currently are legally classified as refugees around the globe. Due to a combination of their geographic locations and policies, some countries have more refugees than others. Currently Lebanon has the highest number of refugees with

19.8 percent of the country's population having refugee status (Norwegian Refugee Council, 2022). This is followed by Jordan (10.4%), Nauru (6.8%), Turkey (5.0%), Uganda (3.7%), Sudan (2.7%), Sweden (2.6%), Malta (2.5%), Mauritania (2.4%), and Greece (2.2%) (Norwegian Refugee Council, 2022).

Students might be surprised to learn that the United States does not rank among the top ten countries that welcome refugees, though the numbers are increasing. While recent restrictions due to COVID-19 limited the number of refugees being resettled to safe locations across the globe, these restrictions have been decreasing. In the United States, for example, President Biden increased the number of refugees to be admitted into the country from 15,000 to 62,500 (Biden, 2021).

With more refugees coming into the country and more people with refugee status across the globe, it is likely that students will hear about the struggles refugees are facing, be it on television, in their communities, or in schools. As such, it is important for teachers to help teens to understand what it means to be a refugee and how this global crisis has impacted individuals around the world. This chapter will build on students' understanding of the difference between someone who is an *immigrant*, a *migrant*, a *displaced person*, an *asylum seeker*, and a *refugee* before introducing the graphic novel *When Stars Are Scattered* (Jamieson, Mohamed & Geddy, 2020), which shares the story of brothers living in Dadaab Refugee Camp in Kenya. Intersections with global poverty, food insecurity, education for girls, and disability allow for a nuanced look at the challenges facing youth around the world.

WHEN STARS ARE SCATTERED

When Stars Are Scattered by Victoria Jamieson and Omar Mohamed is a graphic novel that shares the experiences of co-author Omar during his time in Dadaab Refugee Camp in Kenya, Africa. Omar and his brother, Hassan, were born in Somalia but had to leave their home because it was unsafe. Omar shares what life is like at the refugee camp, where he lives with and takes care of Hassan, who was born with developmental disabilities and is predominately nonverbal.

When the book begins, Omar and Hassan have already been in the refugee camp for seven years. Their father has died in Somalia and they don't know where their mother is. Fatima, a woman in a neighboring tent, has taken on the role of foster mother of the two boys. They are waiting for the war in Somalia to end so they can go back home and find their mother, though ultimately that doesn't happen in the time the book takes place. In addition to the trauma of having lost their parents and their home, life in the refugee camp is very challenging. There is no electricity, they have limited resources, and food insecurity is a daily battle.

School becomes especially important to Omar. It is taught in English, so Omar must learn English in addition to learning the other subjects, like math and history. Omar continues to work hard, study, complete chores, and look after his brother. His goal is to be a social worker, but it is hard to have hopes and goals in the camp where resources are scarce and opportunities are limited.

Omar spent a total of fifteen years in Dadaab Refugee Camp before he and his brother were resettled to the United States. Omar explains in the author's note that he "always wanted to write a book to educate others about my experience as a refugee" (n.d.). The Afterword of the book shares photos of both Omar and Hassan. Omar eventually graduated from University of Arizona, became a citizen of the United States, and achieved his dream of becoming a social worker. He also started a nonprofit organization to help other refugees. Through this nonprofit, Refugee Strong, Omar "organizes trips to Dadaab once or twice a year [where he] . . . delivers books, pencils and lamps to students. Refugee Strong also focuses on helping girls continue their studies by delivering menstrual hygiene products and building restrooms for girls—two major stumbling blocks that keep girls from attending classes." Omar and Hassan reunited with their mother in 2017, eight years after they arrived in the United States.

TEACHING STRATEGIES

Before Reading

Before introducing *When Stars Are Scattered,* teachers might choose to begin with the definition of *refugee* and help students unpack what being a refugee means. Students can discuss what might constitute a "well-founded fear of being persecuted." They can consider how people might be in danger because of their race, religion, and/or nationality as well as what types of social groups or political opinions might result in one's life being threatened. For example, teachers might share the brief NPR story, "With Few Options Left, Afghans Who Helped U.S. Troops Hope for 'a Miracle' to Save Their Families" (Frame, 2021), and then lead students in a reflective writing task where they write their understanding of the news story, their thoughts and feelings, and the questions they still have. Later these questions could be used to inspire personal research and an examination of credible sources.

In furthering a discussion and exploration of terms, teachers might want to turn to The United Nations High Commissioner for Refugees (UNHCR) website, which provides some excellent resources that will assist both teachers and students as they prepare to broach a study focused on refugees. Teachers might want to begin with the "Words Matter" summary table, which clearly and concisely shows the differences among refugees, migrants, asylum seekers, and internally displaced people (UNHCR, Teaching, 2001–2021). This resource also provides short animated videos that share overviews of terms and concepts connected to refugees that will help provide an overview and background on which to build knowledge.

After terms are discussed so that students have the vocabulary needed to discuss refugees, teachers might move on to a brief lesson connected to world geography. With regard to where refugees come from and in which countries they are most often provided shelter, teachers might use a map, creating a visual representation of geographic locations and guiding students in reflecting on why refugees might be more likely to seek asylum in some countries than in others. The UNHCR provides maps that show both from where the majority of refugees come as well as which countries host refugees from specific areas (UNHCR, Origins and Destinations, 2022). As the maps suggest, teachers might have students first make predictions, share the maps, and then lead a discussion regarding if there were any surprises and why.

Finally, teachers might turn to children's picture books as an entry for students to gain more information, insight, and interest in the topic of refugees. While there are a wide variety of children's picture books that portray the refugee experience, teachers might want to focus on nonfiction selections, since *When Stars Are Scattered* is also a nonfiction piece with visual components. For example, teachers might share *Lost and Found Cat: The True Story of Kunkush's Incredible Journey* (Kuntz & Shrodes, 2017), which chronicles an Iraqi refugee family's journey with their cat, Kunkush, to Greece. When Kunkush gets lost, a social media campaign helps reunite the family with their beloved cat. Teachers can lead students in discussions regarding how technology might assist refugees as well as how it might be overwhelming for refugees who have no experience with technology, should they be resettled in a country that largely relies on it in school and work settings.

When I Get Older: The Story Behind "Wavin' Flag" (K'naan, 2012) is another picture book that shares one refugee's experiences before and after he was forced to flee his home. K'naan was born in Somalia and was forced to flee with his mother and siblings when war broke out in their country. The family was eventually resettled in Toronto, Canada, where K'naan has become a well-known poet, singer-songwriter, and rapper. His song "Wavin' Flag" hit number one in nineteen countries and was used as the anthem for the 2010 FIFA World Cup Soccer Tournament.

Picture books, like the above, can provide students with an accessible entry into the topic of refugees in general and personal narratives about refugees in particular. They also help to portray that there is not a single refugee narrative and show students how multiple factors influence each person's experiences. Teachers can guide students in reading news stories about these and other refugees, invite them to listen to K'naan's song and other music by and about refugees (see below), and set the stage for diving into *When Stars Are Scattered*.

During Reading

While students are reading, they might want to keep a list of difficulties that are faced in the refugee camp. Students may be unfamiliar, for example, with how food is distributed in refugee camps. Teachers can ask students: *What are empty days? What are the challenges (besides being hungry) of not having enough food to eat? What are some potential barriers to the refugees getting food?* Teachers can also lead students in considering the challenges of not having electricity, asking students to track the electricity they use in the evenings when they come home from school (e.g., lights, heat, computers, television, charging phones, etc.). Then they can discuss how their lives would be different if they had no electricity as well as the impacts of electricity on daily life such as cooking, cleaning, and receiving medical care.

In the book, when a community leader, Salan, encourages Omar to attend school, his life begins to change. As much of the novel shares Omar's school experiences, teachers might lead students in creating a Venn diagram or other graphic organizer where they compare and contrast schooling in the camp and their own experiences with school. For example, in Dadaab, there are not enough desks for all of the students, so some have to sit on the floor. Girls sit on one side of the classroom, and boys sit on the other. Most of the students don't have paper, pencils, or books, and "sometimes kids faint at school because they are so hungry" (p. 52). In identifying differences, students might begin to consider why these differences exist.

Despite the differences, there are a lot of similarities, too, and it is important for teachers to focus on similarities in order to not inadvertently exclude other refugees. For example, all lessons are taught in English. Students have different classes like history, science, and math. Students can consider questions like: *What constitutes an education? Why should education be a basic human right?*, and *Why do some people so desperately want to go to school while others desperately want to stay home?*

After Reading

After reading, teachers can lead students in a discussion regarding the effectiveness or strengths and weaknesses of the graphic novel format for telling stories. They might ask students: *How do the pictures enhance the story? How do they help you to understand the characters and setting? Does the comic format enhance or detract from the seriousness of the topics addressed? How?; and will you identify an example?* Teachers might lead students in identifying a significant event in their own lives, first writing about it, and eventually creating their own comic version of it. Students could create their own original art, or use clip/electronic art, or photos from magazines for the visuals in their narratives. They might add an Author's Note that shares why they chose the visuals they did.

After writing their own Author's Note, teachers can guide students to read the Authors' Note of *When Stars Are Scattered,* specifically leading them to reflect on Omar's words. He writes:

> Empowering and supporting refugees is key to helping them succeed not only in the camps, but also in their new communities. No one chooses to be a refugee, to leave their home, country, and family. The last thing I wanted in this world was to be a refugee. I have worked hard to overcome my challenges as a refugee, but I would not have been able to do it without the staff of UNHCR, Save the Children, World Food Programme, Care International, Church World Service, the Islamic Community Center of Lancaster, PACRI, and the DSAK Foundation. (Jamieson & Mohamed, 2020, Author's Note)

In addition to these organizations mentioned, Omar also is the founder of Refugee Strong, "which focuses on improving and making education available to all children in refugee camps." Students might choose one of these organizations that Omar mentions or identify other organizations that support refugees and conduct related research, ultimately sharing what they learn with their classmates and, perhaps, communities. They could, for example, create posters/pamphlets with the information they find regarding these organizations and then have a gallery walk where they share what they have created. They might also research to ascertain if their own, or surrounding communities, have organizations that support people who come from refugee backgrounds.

INTERSECTIONS

When Stars Are Scattered offers multiple opportunities for an investigation of other social justice issues including global poverty, food insecurity, disability, lack of/barriers to education for girls, and women's rights. Of particular import in the book is the contrast of life in the camp for boys and for girls. It is so striking that even Omar notices it: "I started noticing that when I'd fetch water before school I'd see some of my classmates there too . . . but only the girls. When I went for walks with Hassan after school, I'd see other kids watching their siblings too . . . but only the girls. Besides Nimo and Maryam, none of the other girls in my block even went to school—they stayed home to do chores" (p. 56). Students can share their opinions regarding the lack of equality, identifying why they think those gender roles exist, and what could be done to change the system.

It is often the case that girls around the globe lack opportunity for schooling. If families cannot afford to send all of their children to school, they most likely will choose their oldest son to go. The book shares the experiences of two of Omar's classmates, Nimo and Maryam, specifically about to their drive to get an education. Nimo tells him:

> Last year our teacher pulled all the girls aside after class and told us that every year, the top students in Kenya can earn scholarships to study at a university in Canada. Refugee kids, too! And girls can get extra help, since it's harder for us to go to school here . . . Maryam and I are going to get those scholarships . . . We just have to stay at the top of our class through high school and we can go!" (p. 84)

Teachers might want to use excerpts from Malala's book *I Am Malala: How One Girl Stood Up for Education and Changed the World* (Young Readers Edition) by Malala Yousafzai and Patricia McCormick alongside a discussion of education for girls, or they might also consider drawing from Malala's website, Malala.org for further investigation of this topic.

"Working for a world where every girl can learn and lead," Malala.org shares information, news stories, research, and resources specific to education for girls around the world. Students might peruse the information on the site, sharing with the class what they have learned, such as that in Ethiopia "47% of Ethiopian girls who start grade one do not make it to grade five" (para. 3) or that "Almost one out of three school-age children in Lebanon are Syrian refugees" (para. 5).

Also housed on the website is Malala's digital publication, *Assembly,* which shares stories written by girls about issues concerning girls specifically and serves as "a platform for girls to speak out about the issues holding them back" (Malala Fund, 2022, para. 9). Students might choose one of the pieces on *Assembly* to read and share in small groups or with the whole class. For example, Amna Quddus's (2022) opinion piece entitled "The Sanitation Crisis Affecting Girls' Education in Rural Pakistan" shares how "one in three schools in Pakistan lack sanitation facilities" (para. 3), and that girls often "must traverse miles outside their school to go to the restroom in open fields, exposing them to sexual harassment, rape, kidnapping, and attacks by snakes and insects. The lack of menstrual hygiene products—coupled with the absence of toilets—makes an already discomforting situation even more tormenting" (Quddus, 2022, para. 3). Quddus goes on to share the work she did fundraising to build "the first sets of girl-friendly toilets across four primary girls' schools in Bahawalpur" (Quddus, 2022, para. 9). This work may inspire students to create their own social action projects (see below).

Another issue developed in the novel largely specific to equality for women is that of child marriage. In *When Stars Are Scattered,* Omar's classmate Maryam is facing an impending marriage, and she is working hard to try to disrupt the union. When Omar asks her if she will have to leave school when she gets married, she explains, "Well . . . that's why I'm studying so hard. My plan is . . . If I stay number one in my class, and do **really** well in my exams at the end of the year . . . my dad will **have** to let me stay in school. He'll see that a scholarship to Canada is worth a lot more money than getting married" (p. 85). Maryam has goals of going to law school and then coming back to the refugee camp to "help refugee girls know their rights" (p. 86). Students might discuss the various barriers to Maryam's goal as well as how girls are often forced into early marriage, like Maryam, in order to help the family. Teachers might ask students questions like: *Why might a family make the decision to have their young daughter get married? What factors might contribute to that decision? How might a family feel like they do not have a choice?* Questions like this can help students to begin to see the complexity of systemic poverty and how often families have to make impossible decisions in their attempts to keep all family members alive.

If students are interested in learning more about child marriages, UNICEF (2022) provides information that is accessible and appropriate for the middle school student, though the topic can be overwhelming to comprehend. Students might create infographics of the information they learn about child marriages, such as the fact that "girls who marry before 18 are more likely to experience domestic violence and less likely to remain in school" (UNICEF, 2022, para. 5).

Issues connected to global poverty, like food insecurity and access to clean drinking water, are other topics clearly explored in the book, and students may want to extend their knowledge regarding living with economic insecurity. Teachers might start by sharing the United Nations "Sustainable Development Goals" and leading some discussion regarding each of the seventeen goals. Students could, for example, identify which of the goals are and aren't being met in Dadaab, the refugee camp where Omar lives. Teachers might encourage students to work in small groups or with a partner, choosing one of the goals and then conducting related research, ultimately sharing the information with the class. They might break down what the goal means, what it is not (provide a negative example), and offer their opinions about the goals, answering questions like: *Do you think this is an important goal? What are some barriers to meeting this goal? What could be done to remove those barriers?* For example, students could choose goal three: good health and well being. They could explore what they think this means, like access to affordable, quality health care, and what it does not mean: not being able to go to a doctor or to get medicine when you are sick. They might identify that access to hospitals and doctors can be a problem in remote locations as well as sick people having the money to pay for health care as being barriers. Then they might brainstorm ways to overcome these barriers. For example, perhaps doctors could have student loan forgiveness if they work in remote communities. Perhaps students could lobby lawmakers for affordable health care options. This brainstorming activity could be used later, as a springboard for ideas when students are engaging in social action projects (see below).

Finally, as Hassan, Omar's brother, is largely nonverbal and also has some developmental disabilities related to his seizures, students might be inspired to learn more about disabilities in general and disability rights, both in the United States and around the world (see Chapter 7 on disabilities). They could also research the variations in treatment of people with disabilities in different countries, especially as they relate to schooling.

IDEAS FOR SOCIAL ACTION

There are many community groups as well as nonprofit organizations around the world that are working to support refugees, and these organizations may inspire students to create their own social action projects connected to the issues illuminated in *When Stars Are Scattered*. Action projects could include awareness campaigns, fundraising events, and/or volunteer opportunities with local, national, and international refugee resettlement organizations.

Students can begin with searching "support refugees" and then looking at news stories that share what individual communities are doing to help new refugees into the country. For example, backpack/quilt initiatives (Lovdahl, 2022) and Restart Kits (Refugee Care Collective, 2022) might inspire students to create some sort of similar welcome bag for new refugees in their schools.

Teachers can encourage students to reach out to local refugee resettlement organizations to identify specific needs, be it school supplies, clothing items, or household items. Students could then, for example, organize a donation day for the needed items, advertising the event throughout the community. They might want to have a donation day in which they have entertainment and food, and share information about refugees in general and perhaps even those in their own community specifically.

When someone is new to a neighborhood, they often need advice on where they can locate specific resources. Students might brainstorm places, organizations, and events in their own community that might be useful for refugees to know, like the library, churches, parks, and community centers. They could then create fliers/booklets for new refugees that share their recommendations and supports for new families in their community. Students might enjoy including their own reviews or pictures along with the information so newcomers can have information on the community, such as where to get houseware items, cultural activities such as free concerts, community theater performances, the fair, and markets that stock specialty foods, spices, etc. from across the globe that newcomers might want to make them feel closer to home.

Finally, students might be inspired to create an awareness campaign, sharing information they have learned about refugees, dispelling myths, and offering suggestions for how to help. They could launch their campaign on social media sites, on the school web page, or through, for example, a weekly information-share on the morning announcements.

In its unique graphic novel format, *When Stars Are Scattered* provides young adults with opportunities to think outside of themselves and perhaps their local communities and to look at issues that are impacting others around the world. Topics intertwined with the refugee crisis like global poverty, education for all, and food insecurities, thoughtfully discussed with classmates and the teacher, can help students to see beyond their immediate contexts and consider what our personal responsibility is to help support those who are more vulnerable than ourselves, if we can.

SUPPLEMENTAL RESOURCES

Connected Young-Adult Literature

Azzi in Between by Sarah Garland
Refugee by Alan Gratz
Everything Sad Is Untrue by Daniel Nayeri
The Red Pencil by Andrea Davis Pinkney
I Am Malala: How One Girl Stood Up for Education and Changed the World (Young Readers Edition) by Malala Yousafzai and Patricia McCormick

Connected Media

"Teaching about Refugees": https://www.unhcr.org/en-us/teaching-about-refugees.html
"Exile Voices": https://maptia.com/reza/stories/exile-voices (photography)

Connected Poems

"Four Poems about the Courageous and Inspiring Journeys of Refugees": https://www.unrefugees.org/news/four-poems-about-the-courageous-and-inspiring-journeys-of-refugees/
"Who Can I Blame?" by Night Jean Muhingabo
"Six of the Best Poems about Refugees": https://interestingliterature.com/2019/06/six-of-the-best-poems-about-refugees/
"Six Refugee Poems: A Unique Insight Into the Life of Refugees and Asylum Seekers": https://www.freedomfromtorture.org/real-voices/six-refugee-poems-a-unique-insight-into-the-life-of-refugees-and-asylum-seekers

Connected Music

"Running: Refugee Song" (World Refugee Project) featuring Gregory Porter and Common
"Shine Your Light" (song by refugees) featuring Ricky Kej, Aditya Narayan, Neeti Mohan, & Salim Merchant
"Under the Same Sun: A Song about the Refugee Crisis" by Lucy Rose, Rae Morris, Jack Steadman, Björn Ågren, & Benjamin Francis Leftwich
"A Safe Place to Land" by Sarah Bareilles
"Aliens" by Coldplay
"Prayer of the Refugee" by Rise Against

REFERENCES

Amnesty International (2022). Refugees, asylum seekers, and migrants. https://www.amnesty.org/en/what-we-do/refugees-asylum-seekers-and-migrants/
Biden, Joe. (2021). Statement by President Joe Biden on Refugee Admissions. https://www.whitehouse.gov/briefing-room/statements%20releases/2021/05/03/statement-by-president-joe-biden-on-refugee-admissions/
Frame, C. (2021). With few options left, Afghans who helped U.S. troops hope for 'a miracle' to save their families. https://americanhomefront.wunc.org/news/2021-09-15/with-few-options-left-afghans-who-helped-u-s-troops-hope-for-a-miracle-to-save-their-families
K'naan. (2012). *When I get older: The story behind "Wavin' flag."* Tundra Books.
Kuntz, D. & Shrodes, A. (2017). *Lost and found cat: The true story of Kunkush's incredible journey.* Crown Books for Young Readers.
Lovdahl, T. (2022 Aug. 02). Help PBS Wisconsin give quilts to refugee children in our state. *PBS Wisconsin.* https://pbswisconsin.org/article/help-pbs-wisconsin-give-quilts-to-refugee-children-in-our-state/
Malala Fund (2022). https://malala.org/

Quddus, A. (2022). The sanitation crisis affecting girls' education in rural Pakistan. *Assembly: A Malala Fund Publication.* https://assembly.malala.org/stories/the-sanitation-crisis-affecting-girls-education-in-rural-pakistan

Refugee Care Collective. (2022). Restart kits program. https://refugeecarecollective.org/restart-kits/

Siegfried, K. (2022). The refugee brief 27 May 2022. *UNHCR.* https://www.unhcr.org/refugeebrief/the-refugee-brief-27-may-2022/

UNHCR. (2022). Origins and destinations. https://www.unhcr.org/6177f76f4.pdf.

UNHCR. (2001–2021). UNHCR teaching about refugees. https://www.unhcr.org/en-us/teaching-about-refugees.html

UNHCR. (2001–2022). What is a refugee? https://www.unhcr.org/en-us/what-is-a-refugee.html#:~:text=%E2%80%9Csomeone%20who%20is%20unable%20or,group%2C%20or%20political%20opinion.%E2%80%9D

UNICEF. (2022). Child marriage. https://www.unicef.org/protection/child-marriage

United Nations. (2022). Sustainable development goals. https://sustainabledevelopment.un.org/topics/sustainabledevelopmentgoals

World Bank. (2022). Poverty and equity data portal. https://povertydata.worldbank.org/poverty/home/

Chapter 5

Indigenous Rights

Teaching related to Indigenous peoples in the United States should be done with care. We suggest that such education be centered around the tribes and history in the text under study and on the local context nearest to where the teaching occurs to provide for authentic, relevant, and accurate learning experiences. We also encourage that such teaching draws as much as possible from resources approved by and/or created by/with Indigenous individuals or officially sanctioned by Native communities. Too often in our history, cultural artifacts and stories have been appropriated and used without permission or told only from a white point of view, and thus we strongly advocate for partnerships with Indigenous communities and sincere efforts to ensure veracity and sensitivity.

The histories of Indigenous peoples are ones fraught with death and destruction at the hands of settlers but are also ones of resilience, family, and celebration from within Native communities. Providing multiple stories is crucial to students' understandings and critical perspectives. As is commonly known, Native Americans existed in the United States long before the arrival of Europeans. Nations lived different lives according to geographic region and tribal affiliation. While history textbooks typically present Indigenous peoples as one entity, this is far from the truth. For example, in the Arctic, the Inuit lived in dome-shaped houses and depended on fishing for subsistence; in the Southeast, the Choctaw relied on farming; and in the Northwest, the Nez Perce engaged in fishing and hunting for food. There are currently 574 federally recognized tribes in the United States and Alaska (USAGov, 2022). And, although the United States government recognized tribes as sovereign nations and allegedly negotiated with them as such, treaties were often broken and not honored as westward expansion took hold and genocide unfolded. Attempts to assimilate Indigenous peoples into white European ways led to the implementation of boarding schools across the country, and Indigenous children were often taken from their families and forced to unlearn their language and cultural ways of being.

And yet, Indigenous peoples throughout the country remain, showing their resilience and vibrant cultures. There are currently 115 Indigenous languages spoken in the United States, and many tribes are making efforts to preserve and revitalize their language despite a lack of resources (Nagle, 2019). Furthermore, "the vocal and visible presence of Native Americans in public office, at the head of companies, at the forefront of calls for social justice, and within local communities dispel . . . colonial myths" (Pluralism Project, 2022, para. 4) that Native Americans have disappeared. Oral traditions and customs are thriving across communities as well.

In this chapter, we focus on the novel *I Can Make this Promise* (Day, 2019) to discuss the social justice issue of Indigenous rights with specific focus on the broader racism toward and social treatment of Native communities but also examining some of the oft-ignored history of Native Americans in the Northwest through the narrative of a young girl's journey into her mother's past.

I CAN MAKE THIS PROMISE

In *I Can Make this Promise* (2019), Christine Day crafts a story based on her own family's experiences in the Northwest. The story centers on Edie, a middle school student, who stumbles upon a box in her attic that holds the key to her family history and tells of her Native American background. Her mother, who was adopted by white parents, is Indigenous but talks little about her childhood, and her father is white. Edie and her two best friends embark on a journey to uncover whom the contents of the box belong to and to learn the identity of the woman in the pictures they find (who has a striking resemblance to Edie). Eventually, Edie's parents share that the woman, her grandmother, was an aspiring actress, Edith Graham, who gave birth to Edie's mother. Edie's mother was then taken from her against her will and placed into an orphanage. Edie learns that her family is Suquamish and Duwasmish from the Sound area in Washington State and that they have a home and land on Indianola that was passed down to her.

During this discovery, Edie also struggles with her friendships with Serenity and Amelia. The three have been exceptionally close up until this point in the book, but they begin to drift apart as they attempt to create a short film for an upcoming festival. Amelia branches out in her friendships to Libby, a girl who has not been nice to Edie. The growing pains of changing relationships are therefore demonstrated as Serenity and Edie remain friends but Amelia leaves their film group. In the end, Serenity and Edie produce a film that incorporates both Edie's heritage and the artistic skills she improves throughout the novel.

TEACHING STRATEGIES

Before Reading

This novel contains many allusions to historical events, people, and policies that teachers will need to explain before and as students are reading to ensure a fuller understanding of the text. First, defining tribal sovereignty and explaining the history of treaties and reservations is crucial. The National Conference of State Legislatures (2013) explains:

> Tribal sovereignty refers to the right of American Indians and Alaska Natives to govern themselves. The U.S. Constitution recognizes Indian tribes as distinct governments and they have, with a few exceptions, the same powers as federal and state governments to regulate their internal affairs. Sovereignty for tribes includes the right to establish their own form of government, determine membership requirements, enact legislation and establish law enforcement and court systems (para. 1).

Helping students become aware that tribes operate as individual nations within the United States is thus necessary as a background to the book's context. The Plateau People's Web Portal (2022) has a collection of videos in which individuals from tribes in the Pacific Northwest explain sovereignty and its implications for them. Students could watch these videos as a class or divide into groups and watch separate ones and share and compare what they learned through a graphic organizer. They might then develop a list of questions about sovereignty within the United States (e.g., related to voting or taxes) and research the answers to those. This can also help with misconceptions of Native communities and rights on reservations.

Again, in order to provide a specific narrative with accuracy and because there is so much diversity among Indigenous communities, we recommend that teachers focus their instruction related to the text on the region it highlights, the Northwest, and use this to expand to the local region as an extension after reading. This will provide localized, authentic knowledge rather than the generalizations that typically accompany Native education. As such, starting with a map (Native Peoples of Washington, n.d.) of Indigenous communities in this area and exploring the geography of the Northwest would provide a visual for students as they read. Having students explore the Sound as well as the location of the tribes around it can show how the beach Edie visits with her family in the text is across from where her family takes her to their inherited land toward the end. It also shows the multitude of tribes around the area, which some students may be surprised to see.

Students could conduct research on the Tulalip tribes, since this is the reservation that Edie visits with her family in the opening of the text. Teachers should emphasize the importance of sources in this type of research, encouraging students to draw on resources that are posted by the tribes themselves or have been created in partnership, rather than sites with unknown authors or without official approval. In pairs, they could select an event on the Tulalip Timeline (2022) to explore and expand upon and could teach the class about their findings, creating an extended timeline as a class that they post on a board or wall in the classroom. They could also explore the websites of the Suquamish (2015) and Duwamish (2018) tribes, viewing their video archives as well as images and reading the information about cultural life in the present, including about their foods and languages. Students could also read about the Letter Writing Campaign (2021) and the Duwamish people's being denied federal recognition and further explore the requirements for federal recognition.

The tribe's websites also introduce readers to Chief Seattle, a figure mentioned in the book, who was a leader in the region, "respected for his peaceful ways, not his prowess at war" (para. 8). The Suquamish site contains a speech he gave in 1854 in response to being tasked to surrender to King George. Teachers could read this with students, asking: *What differences does Chief Seattle point out between his people and the white men? What promises are being made to him, and why does he doubt them? If he agrees to surrender to King George, what are the conditions he asserts must be fulfilled?*

Alleged negotiations with Indigenous tribes should lead to a discussion with students about treaties. The Washington State Office of Superintendent of Public Instruction Tribal Sovereignty Curriculum, called *Since Time Immemorial*, contains a helpful set of lessons (as well as a plethora of additional resources, curated/created in conjunction with local tribes) for introducing students to treaties in the area from this time period (OSPI, 2022). Teachers could expand on the Point Elliot Treaty since it is mentioned in the book, a document that guaranteed fishing and hunting rights to all tribes in the area in the Northwest. The violation of these treaties, however, led to the Fish Wars in the 1960s, for which the National Museum of the American Indian has thorough lessons accompanied by video explanations accessible to middle school students. After much turmoil, the Boldt Decision of 1974 affirmed the tribes' treaty rights to fishing, which teachers may wish to introduce to students as well (Boldt Decision Intro, n.d.). Teachers might ask: *How did the violation of the treaties infringe on Indigenous communities' ways of life? How did the Boldt decision deliver justice to those communities? Why is this decision still important today?*

In addition to this history, teachers can also introduce students to aspects of the social scene that affected Native Americans and are crucial to the book, particularly the representation of Native Americans in film. While the settlers presented Native peoples as savages to be civilized, media perpetuated these stereotypes through popular Western films, often relying on non-Native actors to portray characters. The video, "Indigenous People Review Native American Characters in Film & TV," (2020) contains references to various shows and movies with problematic representations that are critiqued by Indigenous peoples from various communities. The video includes references to the Disney film *Pocohontas*, which students may want to further explore. They could read the Powhatan Nation's statement on *The Pocahontas Myth*, (Horse, 2018) and teachers could ask: *What surprised you, if anything, in reading this statement? Why do you think Disney rejected the Powhatan Nation's offer to assist them in making the story? How does this statement impact the way you think about history?*

During Reading

The book opens with Edie recounting starting kindergarten and realizing she was "different" (p. 1). Her teacher asks "Where are you from, sweetheart? You're such a pretty girl" to which Edie responds, "Seattle," but the teacher pushes, "Yes, that's true. But where are you *originally* from?" (p. 2). Teachers can take the opportunity to explain how this is a common microaggression and explain why this is offensive and isolating to Edie (for teaching about microagressions, see Chapter 8). Addressing the teacher's comment can set the stage for further discussion about racism against Native Americans as it arises at various points in the book. Later, for example, Edith Graham shares in one of her letters that Edie reads, "Every single day, someone walks up to me in the restaurant, or they stop me on the street and ask, 'Where are you from?' At least, those are the polite ones. Just the other day, someone threw a bag of trash at me from their car and drove off laughing" (p. 143). In another instance, Edie's mom describes her own experiences at school: "The kids in my grade used to say I needed a bath, because my brown skin looked dirty to them. They spoke to me in 'Indian' which to them meant wailing and flapping their hands over their mouths. They chased me on their bikes and threw rocks at me" (p. 179). Teachers can ask: *What are some common misconceptions of Indigenous peoples? Where do those come from? Where do we still see these stereotypes and negative treatment of Indigenous peoples?* To expand, teachers might have students read *Five Myths about American Indians* (Gover, 2017) and select one myth about which to reflect and relate in a journal.

In the novel, Edie and her family go to the Tulalip Reservation to buy fireworks. Students will have become familiar with this tribe in their pre-reading activities. Edie asks her mother why "fireworks are banned in our neighborhood," and yet they are "allowed there" (p. 22) on the reservation. Her mother replies, "It's complicated" (p. 23). Given their research in the pre-reading, students could rewrite this dialogue and provide Edie with an explanation that includes their understanding of tribal sovereignty. In this scene at the reservation, Edie sees a woman with a T-shirt that "bears the message 'Find Our Missing Girls,'" and Edie wonders "what that's about" (p. 9). Teachers could explain the issue of *Missing and Murdered Indigenous Women* (We R Native, 2022) to students and have them read about Rosalie Fish, the young runner who became famous for running "in the Washington state high school track meet with a red handprint painted on her face, symbolizing the many Indigenous women who were silenced by violence" (Reyna, 2021). They could also view the video, "Glow Bravely: Rosalie Fish Interview" (2020) where she explains her act of protest as well as her experiences with bullying and mental health.

Throughout the book, Edie searches for information about Edith Graham, whose box of letters, mementos, and photos she discovers in her attic. As she and her friends learn more, they realize Edith "*'must* have been in Hollywood," (p. 37) and feel there is some relation to her mother's adoption. Students could imagine the story of what happened and compose creative pieces that tell the story before they actually learn it later in the book. Teachers could ask students: *Why do you think Edie's parents haven't told her about Edith? What might they be hiding from her, and why? How might they be trying to protect her?*

As Edie and her friends read more of Edith's letters, they learn that she was in fact in Hollywood and was an aspiring actress. Edith shares that she was inspired by "Sacheen Littlefeather . . . the young woman who rejected an Academy Award on behalf of Marlon Brando. I'm still awed by the amount of courage it must have taken . . . it was terribly clever to use that platform to draw attention to Wounded Knee" (p. 87). Students could watch the video of this incident (Oscars, 2008) as well as Marlon Brando's (24floridavideo, 2022) explanation of his choice, which was in protest of the treatment of Native Americans in Hollywood films. Brando had been an activist for Civil Rights issues over the years and was also involved in the Fish Wars, which students would have read about in the pre-reading activities. Over fifty years later, the Academy issued an apology to Sacheen Littlefeather, which students might also learn about through CBC News video (2022). Finally, teachers might explain the reference to Wounded Knee and could use the Digital Public Library's lessons and primary source sets to facilitate understandings of the injustices that happened there. They could ask students: *Why did Brando have Littlefeather speak for him? Do you agree or disagree with his decision, and why? What were the consequences for each of them?* At the end of the book, Edie learns the true story of what happened to Edith and how her mother was forcefully taken. During a trip to Seattle, Edith went into labor and after the "doctor snipped the umbilical cord," he gave her "to a nurse, who darted out of the room without a backward glance" (p. 222). A social worker then came to the hospital and asked a series of questions about Edith, her brother, and her mother and from their responses deemed them "unfit to care" for Edie's mother. She tells Edie, "I was taken away from the hospital and sent to an orphanage" (p. 228). Edie is in disbelief at the "horrific injustice" (p. 230) of this scene, horrified that a child could be removed from its mother. Edith and Theo, however, "knew that state, child welfare, and private-adoption agencies were actively seeking out Native children" (p. 229). Teachers might ask students to consider: *How were the social workers allowed to take children away from families at this time? Why, given the history we have studied to this point, did the government think this was acceptable? How was this a violation of Edith's rights?*

After Reading

Since the adoption is described at the end of the book, students will likely want to research and learn more about this issue in history and the Indian Child Welfare Act of 1978 that was passed in response to it. The National Indian Child Welfare Association (2022) explains the act and its stipulations, noting that "research found that 25%–35% of all Native children were being removed; of these, 85% were placed outside of their families and communities—even when fit and willing relatives were available" (para. 1). Their website also contains a video about a forced adoption after which a child was reunited with his mother. It is important for students to understand the cultural disconnects that allowed the social worker to judge Edith's circumstances as unfit as well as to know that children who are assigned to foster care now must be placed in homes that align with and respect their Native culture.

As an extension, teachers could also engage students with the music and videos of Jayli Wolf, a singer who illustrates firsthand the detriment of forced adoption. Her song, "Child of the Government" and its accompanying music video shows how her father was removed from his family and adopted (Adach, 2021). Recently, some states have tried to challenge the Indian Child Welfare Act and its constitutionality has come before Congress (Locke, 2022). Students could read the arguments against the act and write their own statements either upholding its constitutionality or denying it.

Edith's brother Theo is mentioned throughout the novel. In one of her letters, readers learn, "Theo went to South Dakota in the spring. He joined the Oglala Lakota in solidarity with their cause. Theo has always been greatly involved in activist efforts. I wanted to join him when he protested at our own Fort Lawton, a few years back" (p. 87). Students might research both of these references as well as current protests and controversies underway, such as those around the Dakota Access Pipeline or those calling for the breaching of dams to restore salmon runs in the Northwest (Donovan-Smith, 2022).

Students could compose their own news articles or video reports on the information they gather. Again, teaching discretion in locating reliable resources is advised for such activities.

Finally, students could reflect on their original creative stories on what they expected the story of Edith Graham to be, noting where they may have been on track and where they differed. Since the story ends abruptly, they might write additional scenes in which Edie meets more of her grandmother's family or participates in events with her tribes. They might want to imagine that her and Serenity's video goes viral and brings attention to their local area.

INTERSECTIONS

While the focus of this book is predominantly on Indigenous rights and history, there is some overlap as mentioned above with bullying (see chapter three). In addition, issues around changing friendships are present as Edie navigates changes with Amelia. She describes, "One moment, she's stepping in to help me when I'm panicking in the attic. The next, she forgets to respond to my texts. She'll say that she likes my drawings, but she'll roll her eyes because my ideas for our film are 'too cliché' " (p. 79). This sort of behavior will likely be familiar to middle-grade readers, and teachers can ask: *How do you know when friendships are changing? How can you handle those changes in productive ways? What sorts of qualities do you look for in good friends?*

In addition, divorce is a brief theme in the novel as Serenity shares her experiences with Edie. Serenity tells Edie, "My parents kept the divorce a secret . . . I knew it was happening, and I thought for sure my dad would just . . . [ellipsis in original] *leave*. In the middle of the night" (p. 7). She uses this example to show Edie how sometimes parents keep secrets but with good intentions. Teachers might use this to have students journal in response to: *What situations might adults withhold from their children on purpose? To what extent is this understandable or not?*

Issues of foster care and adoption are central to the novel, and students could examine current laws and policies related to these (see Chapter 9 on foster care). They could further explore the ways that states differ with regard to these issues and discuss their findings across groups. They could research what it takes to become foster or adoptive parents and what the processes are for these.

Finally, clear intersections between treatment of people from Indigenous communities and trauma can be made. According to Dr. Maria Yellow Horse Brave Heart, historical trauma is the "cumulative emotional and psychological wounding over one's lifetime and from generation to generation following loss of lives, land, and vital aspects of culture" (Native Hope, 2018, para. 5).

Teachers might guide students in discussing different types of trauma and identifying historical trauma in conjunction with the novel. They might lead students in activities described in chapter one in order to help them better understand how trauma can impact people and ways in which we can manage trauma, focus on hope, and heal.

IDEAS FOR SOCIAL ACTION

The examples of social action in the book could serve as models for students to conduct their own. Marlon Brando standing up for the misrepresentation of Indigenous peoples in media might provide students a path for exposing current misconceptions and negative portrayals of this group (or another marginalized group about which they feel strongly). They could create campaigns virtually or on posters and share them in the school to debunk stereotypes and correct myths. Theo's activism also provides an avenue for students to follow, as not only did he take up causes for his tribe, but he also was an ally to others. Students might consider how to help a current cause such as the MMIW movement or distribute information about the website to increase awareness.

While the land, especially Indianola, is special to Edie in the text, students might research Land Acknowledgements and locate the one closest to them. They can encourage school administrators and officials to open meetings and assemblies with this acknowledgment. This should be accompanied, however, with greater attention, reverence, and treatment of Native peoples and not merely as a checklist item. If a land acknowledgement does not exist in their area, students could follow the advice of the National Museum of the American Indian who suggest: "reaching out directly to local Indigenous communities and to Native Nations forcibly removed from the area in the past to ask how they want to be recognized" (para. 3). They might extend this to a visit to a local tribe's museum and attend local Indigenous cultural events when they are open to the public.

The issue of coerced adoption is not well known amongst many Americans. To bring greater awareness of this injustice and to ensure the rights granted by the Indian Child Welfare Act are upheld, students might want to host informative sessions or spread knowledge through social media or online videos. The National Museum of the American Indian contains webinars on "Youth in Action: Conversations about Our Future" (2018). Live events are advertised here but past episodes are recorded, so students could organize and host a viewing of any of these to draw on as inspiration as well.

I Can Make This Promise (Day, 2019) is a powerful story with a multitude of opportunities for teaching about Indigenous rights and histories. References in the text and extensions from them can serve to both reflect students' realities and to generate new understandings. Importantly, these have ramifications in history but also extend into the present day, as the struggle for equity and justice persists in Native communities across the country.

SUPPLEMENTAL RESOURCES

Connected Young Adult Literature

Native Women Changing Their Worlds by Patricia Cutright
The Sea in Winter by Christine Day
Charles Albert Bender: National Hall of Fame Pitcher by Kade Ferris
Healer of the Water Monster by Brian Young

Connected Teaching Resources

American Indians in Children's Literature: https://americanindiansinchildrensliterature.blogspot.com/
Techniques for evaluating for American Indian web sites: http://www.u.arizona.edu/~ecubbins/webcrit.html
Tips for Teachers: Developing Instructional Materials about American Indians by Debbie Reese and Jean Mendoza: https://americanindiansinchildrenslitereature.blogspot.com/p/tips-for-teachers-developing.html
Tips for Choosing Culturally Appropriate Native Books and Resources by Cathy Gutierrez-Gomez: https://www.colorincolorado.org/article/tips-choosing-culturally-appropriate-native-books-and-resources

Connected Poetry

"Perhaps the World Ends Here" by Joy Harjo
"Whose Mouth Do I Speak With" by Suzanne Rancourt
"Carrying Our Words" by Ofelia Zepeda
When the Rain Sings: Poems by Young Native Americans

REFERENCES

24floridavideo. (2022). Marlon Brando on rejecting his Oscar for 'The Godfather': The Dick Cavett Show. https://www.youtube.com/watch?v=QeZLYbqv1t4
Adach, K. (2021). Stripped of identity: Powerful music video depicts lasting impacts of sixties scoop. *CBC radio*. https://www.cbc.ca/radio/unreserved/how-indigenous-musicians-are-using-song-to-reclaim-their-identities-1.6000539/

stripped-of-identity-powerful-music-video-depicts-lasting-impacts-of-sixties-scoop-1.6007784
Boldt Decision Intro. (n.d.). Rivers in time project. https://www.k12.wa.us/sites/default/files/public/indianed/tribalsovereignty/high/ushighschool/ushighschoolunit1/level1-materials/boldtdecisonarticleandactivity.pdf
CBC News. (2022). Academy apologizes to Sacheen Littlefeather, who rejected Marlon Brando's Oscar on his behalf. https://www.youtube.com/watch?v=hOcI0M3j9Yc
Day, C. (2019). *I can make this promise.* Heartdrum.
Duwamish Tribe. (2018). https://www.duwamishtribe.org/
Duwamish Tribe. (2018). Chief Si'ahl. https://www.duwamishtribe.org/chief-siahl
Global G.L.O.W. (2020). Glow bravely: Rosalie Fish interview. https://www.youtube.com/watch?v=jan-fF0tonw
Gover, K. (2017). Five myths about American Indians. *The Washington Post.* https://www.washingtonpost.com/outlook/five-myths/five-myths-about-american-indians/2017/11/21/41081cb6-ce4f-11e7-a1a3-0d1e45a6de3d_story.html
Horse, C. R. C. (2018). The Pocahontas myth. https://web.archive.org/web/20180410075910/http://www.powhatan.org/pocc.html
Indigenous people review Native American characters in film & tv. (2020). BuzzFeedVideo. https://www.youtube.com/watch?v=DBBFWH4oSmM
Letter writing action: Protest the denial of tribal recognition for the Duwamish. (2021). https://static1.squarespace.com/static/5ad0f1b9c258b4273c53d08f/t/60df9c8b12c3dd7f79cd49c7/1625267340038/DuwamishLetterWritingPacket2021%2B%281%29+%282%29.pdf
Nagle, R. (2019). The U.S. has spent more money erasing Native languages than saving them. *High Country News.* https://www.hcn.org/issues/51.21-22/indigenous-affairs-the-u-s-has-spent-more-money-erasing-native-languages-than-saving-them
National Conference of State Legislatures (NCSL). (2013). An issue of sovereignty. https://www.ncsl.org/legislators-staff/legislators/quad-caucus/an-issue-of-sovereignty.aspx#:~:text=Janurary%202013,to%20regulate%20their%20internal%20affairs
National Indian Child Welfare Association. (2022). About ICWA. https://www.nicwa.org/about-icwa/
Native Hope. (2018). Understanding historical trauma and Native Americans. https://blog.nativehope.org/understanding-historical-trauma-and-native-americans
Native Knowledge 360. (2018). The fish wars. Smithsonian *National Museum of the American Indian. https://americanindian.si.edu/nk360/pnw-fish-wars#title*
Native Knowledge 360. (2018). Honoring original Indigenous inhabitants: Land acknowledgement. Smithsonian *National Museum of the American Indian. https://americanindian.si.edu/nk360/informational/land-acknowledgment*
Native Knowledge 360. (2018). Youth in action: Conversations about our future. Smithsonian National Museum of the American Indian. https://americanindian.si.edu/nk360/student-programs/recorded-student-webinars

Native Peoples of Washington. (n.d.). Puyallup Tribe's GIS Department. http://puyallup-tribe.com/gis/downloads/NativePeoplesOfWashington_Web.pdf

Oscars. (2008). Marlon Brando best actor Oscar win for 'The Godfather': Sacheen Littlefeather. https://www.youtube.com/watch?v=2QUacU0I4yU

Plateau People's Web Portal. (2022). What does sovereignty mean to you? https://plateauportal.libraries.wsu.edu/collection/what-does-sovereignty-mean-you

Pluralism Project. (2022). *Myth of the 'vanishing Indian.'* Harvard University. https://pluralism.org/myth-of-the-vanishing-indian

Suquamish Tribe. (2015). https://suquamish.nsn.us/

Tulalip Timeline. (2022). *Tulalip Tribes.* https://www.tulaliptribes-*nsn.gov/Base/File/TTT-PDF-38839-Tulalip-Timeline-Mural-20220915-web*

USAGov. (2022). Federally recognized Indian tribes and resources for Native Americans. https://www.usa.gov/tribes#:~:text=The%20U.S.%20government%20officially%20recognizes,contracts%2C%20grants%2C%20or%20compacts

Washington Office of Superintendent of Public Instruction (OSPI). (2022). Middle school unit 1: Washington state history. Territory and treaty making: The point no point treaty. https://www.k12.wa.us/student-success/resources-subject-area/time-immemorial-tribal-sovereignty-washington-state/middle-school-curriculum/middle-school-unit-1-washington-state-history

We R Native. (2022). What is the MMIW movement? https://www.wernative.org/articles/what-is-the-mmiw-movement

Chapter 6

Sexual Orientation And Stigma

With the federal government extending legal recognition of same-sex marriage in 2015, some may feel that the stigma surrounding sexual orientation has lessened. Despite that sentiment, identifying on the LGBTQIA+ spectrum is still difficult in many ways, and the political environment surrounding it remains precarious. Not only does bullying (see Chapter 3) related to sexual orientation often occur in schools, but students who identify as such frequently experience adversity from families and broader society as well. Middle school students are often searching to define who they are, and part of that includes their sexuality. As teachers, we must affirm and value our students' journeys and encourage their acceptance of one another along the way.

We realize, however, that this chapter comes at a time when state legislation threatens the ability of teachers to freely use curriculum related to the topic of sexual orientation. In Florida for example, this became a heated issue in March 2022 when Governor DeSantis signed the "Parental Rights in Education" bill that precluded teachers from including curriculum related to sexual orientation or gender identity from kindergarten through 3rd grade or from teaching about such topics in ways that were not deemed developmentally appropriate for students (Diaz, 2022). Other states have followed suit or are set to do so, including Alabama and North Carolina.

Such contention does not just affect the teachers who must abide by local laws, it also creates a harsh reality for our students. Conron (2020) reported that 1,994,000, or 9.5% of youth ages 13–17 in the United States are LGBTQ. According to the 2019 National School Climate Survey, "59.1% of LGBTQ students felt unsafe at school because of their sexual orientation," and "32.7% missed at least one entire day of school in the past month because they felt unsafe or uncomfortable" (GLSEN, 2020, p. 3). The same students are avoiding school functions, extracurricular activities, bathrooms, and locker rooms due to concerns for comfort and safety. These statistics are deeply saddening, and we must do better to not only increase students' understanding of one another, but to also provide a more inclusive environment in schools where students can fully feel safe to enjoy and experience all that they desire—be it sports, clubs, dances, or other gatherings.

As we noted in the Introduction, we understand that this culture of surveillance that currently exists in our public schools may, rightfully, instill fear in teachers. Yet with the data we have just shared on students' needs, we feel it is unjust *not* to teach related texts and topics. We owe it to all of our students, not just some, to be honored and represented in our classrooms. Learning for Justice has a great list of "Best Practices for Serving LGBTQ Students" (Collins & Ehrenhalt, 2022) and the Gay, Lesbian, Straight Education Network (GLSEN) offers teachers the opportunity to order a "Safe-Space Kit." At bare minimum, we can support our LGBTQIA+ students through our pedagogies and disrupt related bullying when it occurs. In addition, we feel there are ways to teach related curriculum that is "developmentally appropriate" and can achieve the standards in any state. In what follows, we share some of those strategies focusing on the novel *King and the Dragonflies* (2020) and illustrate how teachers can facilitate students' critical perspectives on sexual orientation and stigma in our society as well as foster community and acceptance.

KING AND THE DRAGONFLIES

Callender's powerful novel, *King and the Dragonflies* (Callender, 2020), is set in a small town on the bayou in Louisiana. The main character, a young Black man named Kingston (called King), has lost his brother, Khalid, in a tragic, inexplicable incident. King shares, "Doctors still don't know what happened. Can't figure out why one second, a healthy sixteen-year-old teenager is playing soccer on the field, and the next, he's dead on the ground" (p. 35–36). King thinks his brother has turned into a dragonfly, so he likes to look for them to feel like his brother is near.

The book also traces the story of Sandy, a former friend of King's and a white boy. Sandy runs away from his home where his abusive father, the sheriff, and his brother, Mikey, who is rumored to have killed a Black man, live. Sandy had previously disclosed his sexuality to King one night when they were friends, but Khalid overheard and encouraged King to end their relationship, saying, "You don't want people to think you're gay, too, do you?" (p. 27). Despite the end of their friendship, when Sandy runs away to escape his abusive father, he initially hides in a tent in King's yard. Upon discovering Sandy, King helps him escape to an abandoned building on the bayou and provides him with food. The two rekindle their friendship and talk at length about generational racism and the potential differences in racism and homophobia. A townwide search ensues for Sandy, and he is returned to his father, much to King's dismay. However, in the end, and perhaps with some help from King's parents, Sandy eventually ends up in a safe living situation.

Throughout these events, King struggles to come to terms with his own sexuality. He tries to date Jasmine, a friend at school, but ultimately realizes he does not feel the level of attraction he expects from a romantic relationship. After Sandy is returned home, the sheriff, angry about King's role in aiding Sandy, outs King to his own parents (blaming King for "making" Sandy gay), and King then has to deal with his family's response and potential homophobia. As a Black man, King's father's concerns about King's place in the world are layered, but the book ends with him telling his son he loves him and is trying. As King learns to accept himself, his family also learns to accept the death of Khalid, and the book ends with a feeling of healing and hope. As a whole, Callender (2020) delivers heavy themes and complicated social topics through a text accessible for middle school readers.

TEACHING STRATEGIES

Before Reading

To acquaint students with the terms and labels they will encounter in the book and to prepare them for discussions in class, it is crucial that teachers start with language. The Gay, Lesbian, and Straight Education Network (GLSEN, 2014) has a helpful list of terms with which to begin. In going through these terms, students could mark those with which they are familiar, those they did not know, and any questions they may have. We encourage a welcoming and opening environment, so that students feel comfortable asking questions. We find the assumption that "all individuals are coming from a good place" a valuable approach to such topics, and that when we know better, we can do better. Communicating this to students and setting up a classroom community in advance where students feel secure and are expected to ask questions is important (see Introduction for setting up classroom environment).

In addition to these terms, ensuring that students understand privilege, an unearned social advantage that can come from any dominant group membership (e.g., white, male) as well as heteronormativity, the assumption that heterosexuality is the norm (e.g., men should only like women) are also necessary (UCA, 2017). Especially discerning that these are systemic structures is key, and this can be difficult for students. To facilitate this, teachers might write different systems of privilege on large post-its or online using Jamboard and ask students to place post-its (anonymously) as to what people in those groups might gain through their membership. A few examples to start them off can prompt more participation. For example, under "Ability," an example could be "most buildings are designed for those who can move freely in and out of them." Or, for "English-speaking," an example is "Being able to communicate in the same language with another person in most instances, such as in getting a loan." Brainstorming examples can cultivate students' perceptions of how privilege interacts with systems such as in these—construction or finance.

Furthermore, teachers will want to avoid instilling guilt for having certain privileges, which can often be a pitfall of such education. Kleinrock (2018), a 4th grade teacher, provides a useful perspective on teaching about privilege:

> Privilege is a concept I introduce as a way for them to examine the power they have in certain situations—the power we all have, depending on our identities. It is unfair that some people have privilege while others don't, but I don't teach about it as a reason to feel guilty about one's identity. I want my students to see it as a tool that can be used to elevate others. At the same time, I want them to recognize the injustice that some people have access to resources and opportunities that others don't, based on race, religion, gender, sexual orientation, ability or financial means. (para 7)

After students complete the above activity, they could return to the posters and record ways that people with this privilege could use it to benefit others. For English-speaking, for instance, they could note that others who speak English and another language could become volunteers in situations where translators are needed. Finally, they could also return and add ways the system or structure could change to become more inclusive, such as employing translators or hiring loan officers who speak more than one language. Building from individual to structure shows students the overarching nature of privilege.

Extending upon language, the expression "that's gay," continues to be frequently heard in schools. In fact, on the School Climate Survey (2019), 98.8% of LGBTQ students "heard 'gay' used in a negative way" and "96.9% of GLBTQ students heard the phrase 'no homo' at school" (p. 3–4). Learning for Justice (2022) has a stellar lesson for middle schoolers that promotes reflection specifically on such harmful language and asks them to note what they would do if they heard it. Students could also watch the video "LGBTQ Out Loud Chapter 10: That's So Gay" (2017) with commentary on the phrase and its impact. The video "Find a Different Word" (Choate Smass, 2013) also provides students' and teachers' perspectives on misuse of the word. Along these lines, teachers can share with students how language changes over time and include a list of terms that are outdated or offensive so as to ensure those are avoided in conversation. The GLAAD Media Reference Guide (2022) contains "Terms to Avoid," which includes some with which students may be familiar but not know are offensive, such as "sexual preference," or "gay rights." In debunking these, teachers will enhance their students' literacies and ability to dissect broader narratives often perpetuated in the media. Students might practice finding examples of when these terms are used and rewriting the example to use more inclusive language.

Finally, students will likely have varied knowledge of the history of stigma surrounding sexuality in the country, especially in Louisiana where the book is set. Teachers could have students construct a timeline of the history of LGBTQ Milestones in the United States with a specified number of entries (e.g., 7–10) or they could provide dates and events for students to match up from one such as CNN's (2022) or from Morris's (2009) for the American Psychological Association. It would be especially worthwhile to align these with movements in Louisiana, such as how national activism in the 1970s was felt on a local level. Teachers could assign particular events from these timelines for students to explore with partners as well as create a class timeline.

During Reading

This novel contains a multitude of possibilities for discussing sexuality. In the second chapter, King "outs" Sandy. This happens when his friends are involved in a conversation speculating on Sandy's sexuality, and Camille reports to the group that Sandy was seen in the local library looking at "books for gay people" (p. 23). King then confirms "Yeah . . . he's gay . . . he told me himself once" (p. 23–24). The dialogue continues, with Camille saying "people deserve to know something like that" (p. 24). These are likely feelings that are shared by students in the classroom and are representative of how the public often thinks about sexuality: others have a right to know if a person is not heterosexual. This would be a good point for teachers to engage students in critical reflection, asking: *Why do Camille and Darrell feel they have a right to know about someone else's sexuality? What should a person do if they know and are asked about another person's? How does this example illustrate heteronormativity?*

During this discussion, teachers might lead students through thinking about their own privacy and the rights they have to it. They might share *Sterling v. Borough of Minersville, et al.,* a Federal Appeals Court case which "protects a person's sexual orientation from forced disclosure" (ACLU, 2000, para 2). The decision came after police officers threatened to tell the family of Marcus Wayman, a young man arrested for underage drinking, that he was gay. Wayman went home and died by suicide, and his mother sued the town and the officers. While this case applies to adults "whose professions entrust them with highly sensitive information about young people and sexual orientation" (para. 6), it shows the dire consequences of outing someone and opens dialogue about how individuals should be allowed to disclose details about their sexuality when they wish to do so. Students could read about the court case and related privacy laws to gain insight into the legal and moral ramifications. Further, they could explore the ethics of King's decision, considering: *How did King betray Sandy in that conversation? Why do you think he said what he did in the moment? How else could he have responded?*

In many ways, King acts and speaks in order to seek approval from others. As mentioned, he stopped being Sandy's friend because his brother admonished him upon overhearing Sandy's confession. King revisits Khalid's reaction again and again, saying words such as: "But I know I can't be his [Sandy's] friend, because that's what my brother told me" (p. 26). As he questions his own sexuality later in the novel, he worries about his father's perspective, sharing: "I'd heard him talk about gay people before. I'd heard him say it was *wrong. Unnatural.* Men are supposed to be with women, *because that's just the way it is"* (p. 57). Students can address this issue, with teachers asking: *How might a person's family values go against their own? What should a person do when they want to be friends with someone or do something of which they know their family would disapprove?* Students might journal about a time this has happened to them or about an example from a movie or book they have read, discussing what the issues were and how the situation was resolved (if at all). It will be important for teachers to differentiate this sort of family conflict from parents maybe not wanting their children to associate with people for other reasons. For instance, a mother trying to keep her son away from a group who engages in unhealthy behaviors is different from excluding them based on a category of social oppression, like sexuality.

In his search about his sexuality, King attempts to determine how he would know if he liked Jasmine, his good friend, who identifies as a heterosexual girl. He asks Darell, "How do you know if you like someone–you know, *like that?"* (p. 113), and Darell responds that it's easy. Yet King asks himself, "Jasmine is a friend, and I like her just fine—like her a lot, actually—but should that mean I want to hold her hand? To hug in the hallways . . . should that mean I want to *kiss* her?" (p. 113). Many middle school youth are themselves at a stage where they are wondering similar things, and teachers could lead students through considering: *What are the signs that note attraction to another person? How does a person know the gender to whom they are attracted? How should a person communicate that they are attracted to another? What are King's motivations for dating Jasmine? What are hers? Did King mislead Jasmine?* This might also be a good time for a counselor to visit and hold a workshop with students on attraction, healthy relationships, consent, and responsible behavior.

Despite deciding to date Jasmine, King continues to question his sexuality in the novel. At one point, he admits that he told Sandy in the tent that night, "*I wonder if I might be gay, too*" (p. 150), which lets readers know he may in fact be attracted to the same gender, and in particular, he wonders "about why sometimes, whenever I was around Sandy, my stomach got all funny, and I liked his laugh and his smile" (p. 152). Yet, Sandy and King have very different approaches to their sexuality. On the one hand, Sandy avows, "I'm not ashamed of it. It's not wrong, to like boys instead of girls. I'm not ashamed of it at all, you hear?" (p. 42).

On the other side, King worries about his father, about fitting in, and about what others, like his brother, will think of him. Teachers could use this to show that not everyone's story is the same, asking: *How do the two differ in their approaches to their sexuality? What factors weigh into their diverse paths?* Further, Sandy notes, "But I'm happy I told the truth. I'm happy that I decided to be myself, no matter what. No matter who'll have something to say about it or not. That's what I'm happy about, King" (p. 138). Sandy chooses to tell the truth, rather than to live a lie. Students could discuss: *Who seems better off, King or Sandy? Why? What does each sacrifice in living the way they are in the book?* As an activity, students could write a script of a dialogue between them and either Sandy or King, giving advice at this point in the book that might direct them for the future (for additional activities on self-image and acceptance, see Chapter 3*)*.

After Reading

Fortunately, the book has a hopeful ending. King's parents love him and accept him for who he is, Sandy's father is arrested, and Sandy is relocated to a safe home with his brother. This is a positive message for student readers, and they can reflect on how and why things turned out the way they did. To do so, they could go back and mark instances in the text that impacted the positive direction for each character. For instance, they might note that King's parents were helpful in getting Sandy away from his abusive father. Once they have recorded these instances, they can label the influence: *Was it a peer, an adult, or the individual themselves who helped?* It is important for youth to know that they can ask for help; they do not need to struggle alone with abuse, acceptance, bullying, etc. Ultimately, students can then use this as a springboard for social action (see next section).

The dragonfly is an important symbol in the novel. Students could research facts about dragonflies as an insect as well as its deeper meanings and then conduct their own artistic renderings that depict what they think it might represent in the novel. Their illustrations could answer: *Why would Callender choose a dragonfly to stand for Khalid in the novel? What attraction did King have to them? What other symbol do you think might have worked as well, and why?* After developing their own thoughts, they can watch the video with the author (2021) in which they briefly discuss what the dragonfly means and how it relates to the text as a whole.

In revisiting King's character, students might develop visuals of his growth throughout the novel. In the beginning, King experiences internalized homophobia. He outs Sandy and projects a belief that being gay is bad, even though he inwardly knows he is being "ignorant" (p. 32). Students could discuss this notion of internalized oppression and research it on their own, developing understandings of how it impacts people and manifests according to different identities. They could return to the systems of oppression in the before-reading activities above and explore what the internalization of one of those systems might look like. For instance, internalized misogyny can be seen in a woman who tells herself she's being too aggressive if she's being assertive, or internalized ableism can be seen when a person with a disability believes they are inferior. These internalizations can also play out against others, such as a woman who says that other women cannot succeed in leadership positions because they are too emotional, therefore embodying sexism.

Beyond this focus on oppression, another direction to examine with students could be how subjugation occurs through curriculum. Kacen Callender, the author, has spoken at length about the need for representation in books, especially of queer Black youth. Students might examine the infographic created by Huyck and Dahlen (2019) as a start to the conversation and conduct their own research to delve further into other categories, including sexuality, gender, and ability. They could discuss: *Why do you think the dominant representation in literature is straight, white and male? How could we get more representation into our classrooms? What texts do you wish we had that we don't?* In this way, students are involved in thinking about curriculum and their critical literacies are enhanced.

Finally, King and Sandy engage in dialogue about generational cycles of racism throughout the novel. Sandy admits, "My grandad was a racist. My dad—he says a lot of things he shouldn't. I can't do anything about that . . . but I can still be sorry for it . . . I'm sorry that my family has hurt a whole bunch of people in this town for no reason at all. It's wrong" (p. 133). While again, the goal is not to make students feel guilty for having privilege, what Sandy says here opens a powerful door for having students think about generational oppression and ways to work against it. Teachers could ask students here: *Why does Sandy apologize for something he didn't do? What can we do about things that happened before us that we know were wrong? What can organizations in society do?* Returning to their timelines from the before-reading activities above, students could generate ideas about how

LGBTQIA+ individuals have been historically harmed or marginalized and think of this in terms of Sandy's apology, considering: *What could be done now to address some of those wrongs?*

INTERSECTIONS

Callender's (2020) text relies heavily on the intersection of race and sexuality. As mentioned above, King feels that he cannot be gay because of both his brother's and father's perspectives. His father especially connected his opinion to race; King shared, "for my dad, this rule was especially true for Black boys like me" (p. 57) and that his father felt, "'If a Black person is ever gay, it's because they've been around white people too much'" (p. 57). For King's father, Black men in the United States already have enough pressure on them that being gay on top of that created more potential problems. Teachers could ask: *Why does King's father feel the world will be harsher on him for being Black and gay? How could his own life experiences affect the way he sees these issues? What does he mean when he says this about white people in this quote?* Teachers will have to take care to navigate students around ideas of the myth of "reverse racism" (Blay, 2015; Sensoy & DiAngelo, 2012) and rather to help them discern how King's father's reaction is based on years of social marginalization.

Students might watch the TEDx Youth video "Rewriting Masculinity" in which Douglas Powell (2020) speaks at length about toxic masculinity. Students could relate certain points from the video to the text. For instance, Powell describes his battle with depression and how men are not supposed to show emotion; this relates well to King and his father's struggle with emotions after Khalid dies. He also references homophobia as related to masculinity and how fathers are scared of that for their sons, which clearly relates to King. His explanations in the video might help clarify for students the dynamics in the book.

Relatedly, a repeated theme in the book is the notion of competing systems of oppression. Sandy is gay, white, and comes from a racist family. King is a Black male whose family has been on the receiving end of racism. Sandy compares King's potential homophobia to Sandy's family's racism, saying: "You think my grandad is bad because he was a racist. But what you're doing, King? You're doing the same. Exact. Thing" (p. 94). In this statement, Sandy equates the two, being prejudiced toward gay people and being prejudiced toward Black people. Later, King reflects and asks: "I think about Sandy. The way he said he gets the same kind of hate. What about him? Does the world fear him? Is it different because people can see the color of my skin, but no one can look at Sandy and see who he loves? And what about who I love?"

(p. 103). Here, King wonders if the visible aspect of his oppression makes it somehow worse. Teachers could challenge students to understand the two perspectives: *How are racism and homophobia alike and different? How might they be experienced similarly and differently by individuals in those groups separately and together (e.g., white and gay, Black and gay)?*

Teachers can define the term "intersectionality" for students and have them note how the two systems that King embodies overlap and why this would cause concern for his father. Hancock's (2011) short video on "Oppression Olympics" and "intersectionality" could illuminate for students the notion of interlocking systems as well as the encouragement to avoid saying that one system is worse than another. Much of the scholarship in this area emphasizes that this is unproductive and divides marginalized groups and pits them against one another, distracting us from actually addressing the real issues and the broader systems that subjugate them in the first place. Students therefore might research the notion of "Oppression Olympics" on their own and be tasked with articulating what it is and why it is not a useful strategy.

Finally, Sandy's dad's abuse is another intersection in the novel that requires attention with readers. While his abuse spans beyond his son's sexuality, we learn that it comes to a breaking point when Sandy stands up to his father about his true self. King shares at one time, "Jasmine whispered to me once that she thinks Sandy's dad might be abusive. She said she wanted to tell a teacher, but she was afraid Sandy would be mad at her" (p. 96). People seemed to know, therefore, but as Sandy says when King asks him about why he had not pursued action, Sandy responds, "He's the *sheriff"* (p. 135), denoting that his father's powerful position makes it difficult for him to conceive of getting help. Teachers could have students research how to find assistance in an abusive situation. They could invite the school counselor as well as local organizations who support abused families to provide information for students. With this knowledge, students could then discuss: *What could Jasmine and King have done to support Sandy if they felt he was abused? What ultimately led to Sandy's change in his home environment? Why is it harder to address abuse by a person in power?*

IDEAS FOR SOCIAL ACTION

Many of the activities and discussion questions described in the previous sections lead easily to social action projects. Students could design a campaign around language use from what they discovered before reading, including words to use and those *not* to use and why. Educating others on offensive expressions such as "that's gay" could help with school culture. They might select one phrase in particular or a set around any system of oppression they discussed. They could also design an action based around their brainstorming for ways to disrupt and change a system of oppression, such as hiring translators. They could then write to the appropriate leaders, depending on the system and the change they constructed, and encourage them to consider their ideas.

After seeing the infographic on the lack of diversity in children's literature, students could create their own infographics on a related topic—again choosing any category of representation and researching it either in books, film, television, etc. and presenting their results. They might do an investigation of their school or local library collections to see how they fare with regards to representing diversity. If they find an area lacking, they might write a letter to the school and/or library boards requesting additional titles be purchased to help close any gaps in representation. Upon noting the influential forces in King's and Sandy's lives (peers, parents, etc.) they could pick a group for which to create a PSA or an informational brochure on how to help a person struggling with an issue, such as their sexuality. For instance, they might make suggestions for parents if their child comes out to them.

Students could use the Powell (2020) TEDx talk as inspiration for debunking common tropes related to masculinity (or femininity, etc.), fashioning their own TED talks and filming them for a screening night at the school. They might also spread awareness on healthy relationships—be those friendships, romantic involvements, or dynamics with parents—either in the form of a poster campaign, through social media, or through a website. If a Genders and Sexualities Alliance (GSA), or similar club does not exist in their school, students could create one. They could also petition for teachers to engage in Safe-Zone training (2022) to have adult advocates in their school. They could elect class officers to hold similar training sessions for peers to educate individuals and generate an inclusive school culture. As a whole, *King and the Dragonflies* provides a number of opportunities for students to act not only on the stigma surrounding sexuality but also on various systems of oppression and their intersections.

SUPPLEMENTAL RESOURCES

Connected Young Adult Literature

Rick by Alex Gino
Darius the Great Is Not Okay by Adib Khorram
Almost Flying Jake Maia Arlow

Connected Music

"Follow Your Arrow" by Kacey Musgraves
"Same Love" by Macklemore & Ryan Lewis (ft. Mary Lambert)
"HIM" by Sam Smith
"You Need To Calm Down" by Taylor Swift
"Rain On Me" by Ariana Grande and Lady Gaga

Connected Media

Gender and Sexuality: Poems for Teens, https://poets.org/text/gender-and-sexuality-poems-teens
NFL Star Carl Nassib Talks about Decision to Come Out. Good Morning America, https://www.youtube.com/watch?v=7G5A97Gc-9s
What Does it Mean to be Black and Queer? by India Hosten-Hughes, https://www.stonewall.org.uk/about-us/news/what-does-it-mean-be-black-and-queer

REFERENCES

ACLU. (2000). Court rules that tragic police outing of gay teen violated constitutional rights; ACLU sees broad impact. https://www.aclu.org/press-releases/court-rules-tragic-police-outing-gay-teen-violated-constitutional-rights-aclu-sees

Blay, Z. (2015 August 26). 4 "reverse racism" myths that need to stop. Huffpost. https://www.huffpost.com/entry/reverse-racism-isnt-a-thing_n_55d60a91e4b07addcb45da97

Callender, K. (2020). *King and the dragonflies*. Scholastic Press.

Callender, K. (2021). Kacen Callender: National book festival 2021. *AdLit: All about adolescent literacy*. https://www.adlit.org/profile/kacen-callender

ChoateSmass. (2013). Find a different word. https://www.youtube.com/watch?v=hk5xdVxqWYU&t=145s

Collins, C. & Ehrenhalt, J. (2022). Best practices for serving LGBTQ students. *Learning for Justice*. https://www.learningforjustice.org/magazine/publications/best-practices-for-serving-lgbtq-students

Conron, K. J. (2020). LGBT youth population in the United States. UCLA School of Law Williams Institute. https://williamsinstitute.law.ucla.edu/wp-content/uploads/LGBT-Youth-US-Pop-Sep-2020.pdf

CNN. (2022, August 11). LGBTQ rights and milestones fast facts. https://www.cnn.com/2015/06/19/us/lgbt-rights-milestones-fast-facts

Diaz, J. (2022 March 28). Florida's governor signs controversial law opponents dubbed "don't say gay." National Public Radio. https://www.npr.org/2022/03/28/1089221657/dont-say-gay-florida-desantis

Gay, Lesbian, and Straight Education Network (GLSEN). (2014). GLSEN key concepts and terms. https://www.glsen.org/sites/default/files/2020-04/GLSEN%20Terms%20and%20Concepts%20Thematic.pdf

Gay, Lesbian, and Straight Education Network (GLSEN). (2020). 2019 National school climate survey: Executive summary. The experiences of lesbian, gay, bisexual, transgender, and queer youth in our nation's schools. https://www.glsen.org/sites/default/files/2020-10/NSCS-2019-Executive-Summary-English_1.pdf

Gay, Lesbian, and Straight Education Network (GLSEN). (2022). GLSEN: Safe space kit. https://www.glsen.org/activity/glsen-safe-space-kit-solidarity-lgbtq-youth

GLAAD. (2022). GLAAD media reference guide (11th ed). https://www.glaad.org/reference/terms

Hancock, A. (2011). What are the Oppression Olympics? USC dornslife faculty: 60 second seminars. https://www.youtube.com/watch?v=kFhCJqmWxkY

Huyck, David & Dahlen, S. P. (2019). Diversity in children's books 2018. https://www.dropbox.com/sh/7zn21ogbx7hrvko/AADB87N9rK1qmQn-sMCdUXa5a?dl=0&preview=DiversityInChildrensBooks2018_8.5x11_f_o.pdf

Kleinroch, E. (2018 March 8). Destigmatizing privilege. *Learning for Justice*. https://www.learningforjustice.org/magazine/destigmatizing-privilege

Learning for Justice. (2022). What's so bad about 'that's so gay'? https://www.learningforjustice.org/classroom-resources/lessons/whats-so-bad-about-thats-so-gay

LGBTQ Out Loud. (2017). Chapter 10: That's so gay. https://www.youtube.com/watch?v=DPBNJrU8YIA

Morris, B. J. (2009). History of lesbian, gay, bisexual and transgender social movements. American Psychological Association. https://www.apa.org/pi/lgbt/resources/history

Powell, D. (2020). Rewriting masculinity. TEDxYouth@RVA. https://www.youtube.com/watch?v=vqHvEFKXUCA

Safe Zone Project. (2022). Resources. https://thesafezoneproject.com/resources/

Sensoy, Ö. & DiAngelo, R. (2012). *Is everyone really equal? An introduction to key concepts in social justice education.* New York, NY: Teachers College Press.

University of Central Arkansas (UCA). (2017). Privilege . . . what does it mean? https://uca.edu/training/files/2017/11/Privilege-What-Does-It-Mean-Handout.pdf

Chapter 7

Access And Disabilities

All people are just temporarily able-bodied. At some point in our lives we will all experience challenges with our physical and/or cognitive health. According to the United States Census Bureau (2022), 40.8 million people (12.7%) had a disability in 2019. Current K-12 students are attending school after the passing of Public Law 94–142, The Americans with Disabilities Act, which called for students to be educated in the "least-restrictive environment" and resulted in the full inclusion of students with disabilities into the general-education classroom being more and more prevalent. However, many students still claim to not know much about nor have experiences with people from various disability groups (Gargiulo, 2009).

    The Society for Disability Studies' mission "seeks to augment understanding of disability in all cultures and historical periods to promote greater awareness of the experiences of disabled people, and to advocate for social change" (Society, 2022). This change cannot happen if people do not educate themselves regarding both what it means to live with a disability in the United States today and why this knowledge is valuable. As such, it is important for youth to investigate systemic barriers in society that could potentially limit those with disabilities to freely and easily live their lives. Says Davidson (2006), "If we think of disability as located in societal barriers, not in individuals, then disability must be seen as a matter of social justice" (p. 126). A unit focusing on disability, therefore, clearly connects to social action that students can enact in their communities. While there are a variety of wonderful middle-level books that feature characters with both visible and invisible disabilities, this chapter will use the book *A Time to Dance* (Venkatraman, 2015) to explore physical disability and concepts from disability studies scholars. Displaying intersections with global poverty, mental health, and women's rights, this novel will provide opportunities for teachers to lead students in identifying local and global issues they want to investigate as well as actions they can pursue to raise awareness and support others.

A TIME TO DANCE

Written in verse, *A Time to Dance* shares the story of Veda Venkat, a dance prodigy in India, whose life and body are drastically altered in a short moment. Veda is a star student and award-winning dancer of the traditional Indian Bharatanatyam dance. In fact, as the book opens, she has just made it to the finals of the Bharatanatyam dance competition. Veda wins the competition, but when she is riding home, the van gets into an accident that kills the driver and seriously injures Veda. She must have her leg amputated below the right knee. Veda struggles with the loss of her limb and her future dreams of being a dancer. As she is in the hospital healing, a doctor of prosthetics meets with her, eventually building a leg for her that will enable her to dance again. Veda struggles physically, mentally, and emotionally as her dance teacher no longer wants to instruct her, she switches to a new dance school, and she starts all over with the youngest girls, relearning the dance she loves.

Through friendships, old and new, loss of loved ones, and a newfound joy for dancing and what she can express through this art form, Veda begins to heal, not just physically, but emotionally and spiritually as well. *A Time to Dance* shows that lives can be changed in an instant, and that while physical disability may result in having to do things differently than their able-bodied peers, humans are resilient, strong, and able to cope with and heal from trauma and loss.

TEACHING STRATEGIES

Before Reading

Teachers might want to start a unit focused on disabilities with some vocabulary and history of disability in our country. While this novel focuses on physical disability, it is important that students know that there are a variety of disabilities, both visible and invisible. Starting with the disability categories that are used in schools, teachers might present an overview of the different disability groups. The U.S. Department of Health and Human Services' Centers for Disease Control and Prevention (n.d.) website gives some definitions, types of disabilities, and statistics regarding disability. Teachers might refer students to this website and have them explore it, identifying: *What are ten pieces of information you have learned? What are five questions you have now? What are three related topics you want to learn more about?*

The United Spinal Association has a one-page handout on Disability Etiquette that can be another helpful place to start a unit on disability access. For example, the handout offers advice on terminology including things like "Avoid saying handicapped, crippled, physically-challenged, differently-abled, wheelchair bound, victim, sufferer; instead use language that the person prefers—this may be person first (person with a disability) or identity first (disabled person). Just ask" (para. 5). Similarly, the National Youth Leadership Network (2006) has a great resource on what language to use and to avoid when talking about disability that students can explore.

Once an understanding of what disability is and how to talk about it has been established, teachers might guide students in looking further into specific types of disabilities. The HIE (2018) website provides a variety of lesson plans and activities connected to living with a disability. In addition to each activity, a link to a YouTube video is provided that can be shared with the class. For example, in conjunction with the lesson on wheelchair users is a short video of an interview with Stephen Hawking. Another lesson shares a video of professional surfer Bethany Hamilton and a third spotlights Orlando Bloom and learning disabilities. Teachers might choose specific videos to share with the class or provide a list of the links, allowing students to choose which video they might like to watch and then tasking them with conducting further research on the individual in the video and/or the disability presented.

In addition, as the novel *A Time to Dance* takes place in India, and the protagonist is a Bharatanatyam dancer, some background on Indian geography, culture, and dance will be necessary for students to clearly understand the book. Maps can be used to identify places mentioned in the book like Chennai, Bangalore, and Rajasthan. An internet search of "Bharatanatyam dance" will yield multiple results. Teachers might show, for example, the winner of the Angikam International Bharatanatyam Dance Competition (Niketon, 2020) or perhaps a video of a dancer closer to their own age such as eleven-year-old Sreelakshmi Makreri (Girish, 2018). Students might want to view a variety of videos and identify what the dances have in common and what makes each unique.

Finally, as with Chapter 9 on *Locomotion* (Woodson, 2003), this novel is written in verse, so teachers might want to review poetry terms with students and lead discussion regarding questions like: *How are books written in verse different from those written in narrative format? What are the strengths and challenges of each format? What do you like and dislike about each format? Why do you think the author of* A Time to Dance *may have chosen the novel in verse format?*

During Reading

At the start of the book, the reader learns that while Veda wants to spend her life dancing, her mother has different dreams for her daughter's future:

> All my life, Ma's been
> Hoping
> I'll do well at science and mathematics
> So I could end up becoming what she wanted to be:
> an engineer.
> All my life, I've been
> Waiting
> For her to appreciate my love
> Of the one thing I excel at:
> Bharatanatyam dance. (pp. 9–10)

Teachers might lead students in a discussion regarding the tensions between doing what you want to do and doing what others want you to do. They might ask: *How do you manage other people's expectations for you? Is there a way for Veda to pursue both her and her mother's dreams? Should she? Why?*

Immediately after Veda wins the competition, people are looking at her with admiration. She says:

> I once read an article about beauty in a magazine
> I measured my nose to see if it was long enough,
> if my lips were thick enough
> to be beautiful
> They weren't. (p. 24)

This passage can lead into a discussion about "beauty," with teachers asking questions like: *What is beauty? What is beautiful to us? What does the media tell us is beautiful? Who gets to decide what is beautiful? How can ideas about beauty be harmful to children? How can we disrupt the messages about beauty that are presented in popular culture?* Further, students might peruse magazines, tracking what is presented as "beautiful" or "masculine" or "feminine" or "strong" (see Chapter 3 for teaching about media representations of beauty). They could even create their own magazine with images of what they feel are examples of beauty.

As they progress in the book, readers learn that Veda's mother was disowned by her family when she married Veda's father:

> Paati told me they disowned Ma when she married Pa,
> even though he was Brahmin
> and they were a lower caste
> because he was a poor librarian
> with no prospects of getting rich
> and they were wealthy. (p. 66)

In order to better understand the caste systems in India, teachers might want to provide some background information to students. The Asia Society (2022) provides a strong overview as well as multiple related resources, and those focused on teaching global competence are free for educators.

In the chapter titled "Strong," one of Veda's dance students says, "My big brother said, Strong boys do sports. Real boys don't dance" (p. 255). Veda responds, "He's wrong, Roshan. Strong boys are brave enough to fight for what they want. Strong boys care about Karma and what's right, not following the crowd" (p. 255). This passage offers an opportunity for teachers to discuss stereotypes with students, especially those based on gender identification. Teachers can ask questions like: *Who gets to decide what it means to be a "boy" or a "girl?" Why are some activities associated with certain genders? What are examples of people who break these stereotypes? What are some other ways we can disrupt gender role stereotypes?*

After Reading

After completing the novel, teachers might share other first-person narratives from people with disabilities. For example, Adrianne Haslet-Davis, once ranked third in the world in ballroom dancing, shares her story of being a Boston marathon bombing survivor and discusses how sometimes people don't know what to say, or say terrible things to those with disabilities, injuries, and/or chronic illnesses, noting: "Words will stay with me forever" (Spectrum O&P, 2022). Adrianne shares her advice for what to do and say when someone is going through the unimaginable. For example, it is important to know the stages of emotions, to be present with someone, and to be their friend (Spectrum O&P, 2022). Students might want to read the article about her experiences, listen to her talk, and/or search for examples of her dancing before and after the accident.

Students might be inspired to research the dancers with disabilities that are mentioned in the novel, such as:

> He's an African-American tap dancer.
> They called him Peg Leg Bates. He danced with a wooden leg
> Way back in the 1920's and '30's.
> Next, Jim shows me an Indian man named Nityananda,
> Dancing a classical style similar to Bharatanatyam . . .
> But it's the third dancer
> off whom I can't take my eyes:
> a dark-haired, round-faced Indian lady.
> 'Sudha Chandran,' Jim says.
> She danced your own beloved Bharatanatyam

> With a simple, inexpensive artificial limb
> Created in India the Jaipur foot. (p. 95)

If dancers are not interesting to students, they might want to research other athletes in sports that they do love, like Bethany Hamilton who survived a shark attack and ultimately returned to professional surfing. Hamilton offers a variety of resources available for free on the internet on topics such as surfing, surviving, and staying motivated, and students might want to learn more about her or other similar athletes' experiences. Alternatively, students might want to investigate technology connected to helping those with physical disabilities. From prosthetics, to wheelchairs, to thirteen-year-old Jordan Reeves's invention of a prosthetic limb that shoots glitter (Born Just Right, n.d.) students can see trends in technology and ways in which STEM fields can help support those with medical needs.

As another related research opportunity, students might search the history of the International Paralympic Games, which started in 1960, tracing the evolution of the event, the number of countries and athletes involved, and winners and records throughout the years (International Paralympic Committee, n.d.). They might compare the structure and format of the games along with the events in which athletes can participate with the International Olympic Games. Students might choose to research a certain year of the games to study, either the winter or the summer Paralympic Games, or to investigate a specific event of the paralympic games or specific athletes. They can share the information they learn with the class, and then the class can consolidate and synthesize the information, creating either their own infographic, documentary, or bulletin board to share with classmates, family, and community members.

In the chapter titled "Names" readers get a glimpse into the strong friendship between Veda and Chandra. Veda says:

> "Friendship is about laughing when the other person is joking to
> make you feel better
> Even if you don't find her joke all that funny" (p. 87).

To help students consider what it truly means to be a friend—in good times and bad—as well as the small acts they can do to foster and strengthen friendships, teachers might have students create their own "Friendship is . . . " mural for the classroom or school or perhaps create a "Friendship is . . . " picture book, with each student creating one page. The book could then be shared with elementary students and/or placed in the school library for others to check out. Similarly, at the end of the novel, Veda is performing at a dance festival. Before she performs she "bow(s) to the crystal symbolizing

God as the fragmented light within us that strengthens through each compassionate act as our souls progress from one life to the next" (p. 306). Teachers can guide students in brainstorming their own list of "compassionate acts" that they can practice in the classroom, at school, in their homes, and in their communities. They can refer to Chapter 8 for ideas of small acts of kindness they can share with others.

While this book focuses on disabilities connected to mobility, there are, of course, other disabilities that students might want to research. They can refer to the list of definitions and descriptions presented at the beginning of the unit, and choose a different disability to research. They might consider the history of that disability—when it was identified/named, supports available and famous people living with the disability. They can investigate their school and community to make sure all are included and have the access needed to fully participate in whatever it is they want to pursue. If barriers are identified, students can brainstorm ways to break those barriers in order to create more inclusive environments for all.

Finally, as this is a novel in verse, teachers might have students further explore the effects of this form through either rewriting a chapter of the novel in the narrative format, or writing about an event in their own life in the verse format (see also Chapter 9).

INTERSECTIONS

A Time to Dance offers strong intersections with global poverty, access to health care, bullying, and managing trauma. Mr. James is a doctor from the United States who "is collaborating with an Indian research team to create cost-effective modern prostheses" (p. 53). Students might investigate barriers to health care on a global scale as well as efforts to help those who don't have financial means to access the health care they need. For example, students might look to the website doctorswithoutborders.org to read more about current medical crises around the globe, like cholera in Haiti (4 Oct. 2022), Ebola in Uganda (5 Oct. 2022), and malnutrition in Nigeria (27 Sept. 2022). They might create a map of the world, indicating where the greatest global health crises are located, what might be some causes of the problem, and ideas for how to help. Similarly, they might research the nonprofit Vision to Learn (2022), which provides eye examinations and glasses to children at no cost.

Throughout the book, Veda also has to deal with bullying from her classmates:

"Hey, Veda, I was pretty lame today. Wasn't I?" She giggles.

> Her twin, Meghna, peals with laughter.
> As they walk away, I hear Mekha say,
> "Veda's so sensitive!
> Are we supposed to stop using certain words
> because she's handicapped?
> Should we give cricket stumps
> a new name now that she has a stump?"
> The girls fall on each other, laughing some more,
> and their taunts echo loudly in my head
> long after I leave the field. (p. 85)

Teachers might refer to Chapter 3 for ideas on how to facilitate discussions on and activities regarding bullying. In addition, Lora Rozler's (2018) Words Hurt! post on the Words on a Limb blog shares several activities that teachers can use with students that focus on the power that words have to both harm and heal. Referring to the Before Reading activities, teachers can remind students of what expressions should not be used regarding people with disabilities and why. They might extend this into a lesson about microaggressions (see Chapter 8) and how everyday expressions, even without malicious intent, might actually cause harm to an individual. They could generate scenarios of what a person could do if they overhear a microaggression particularly related to disability and how they might interrupt the negative messages.

Finally, as the novel centers on healing from trauma, discussion, questions and activities shared in Chapter 1 are applicable to this chapter as well. For example, teachers might lead students through some breathing activities, or like the book describes, in practicing some yoga poses or using other forms of art to center themselves and to find peace. They might research other strategies for coping with trauma and write a letter to Veda in which they encourage her and suggest techniques they have learned or ones that help them.

IDEAS FOR SOCIAL ACTION

There are a variety of social action projects connected to disability that students might be inspired to enact. They might, for example, look at accessibility of buildings, parking lots, structures, resources, and entertainment for people with disabilities in their own communities (e.g., close captioned movies, braille signs, accessible entertainment venues). If they find barriers to access, they can alert the public to these barriers through letters to the editor or social media campaigns. Moreover, students can explore how engagement in the arts can help people find some relief and heal from trauma. Social action projects may include an investigation of opportunities to engage in the arts in students' own communities and taking steps to identify and break barriers to those resources and opportunities. For example, students might take a walking tour of their school and their community, noting recreational places and spaces, especially those for children, that are accessible and those that are not. Does their town have, for example, accessible playground equipment at the local park? If they identify places and spaces that need more accessibility, they might be inspired to write a letter to the newspaper, or propose their ideas to a city council or school board meeting.

Born Just Right is the nonprofit started by Jennifer and Jordan Reeves. They also founded the Unicorn Project, a prosthetic arm that shoots glitter. Students might want to explore the site and find ways to support this organization that focuses on advocacy for children. In fact, there are numerous nonprofits that offer supports and services for people with special needs and their families. Students might want to research organizations like Easter Seals, The Special Olympics, and/or similar groups. Further, students might look to their own communities to see what organizations and supports are available for people with disabilities. They might compare organizations' missions, use of funding, allocation of resources, etc., and then choose the organization they feel most compelled to support. Students can conduct a fundraising event with donations going to their chosen organization. They could also, for example, screen a film that has characters with disabilities, like *Finding Nemo* or *How to Train Your Dragon*, and have a pre-viewing discussion regarding what to look for in authentic and respectful portrayals of disability and a question and answer session afterward.

Students might want to do a search of their school or local library to see how many children's and middle-level books that portray characters with disabilities are available. They might compare their list with lists of Schneider Family Book Award and Dolly Gray Book Award Winners to determine how many award winning books that represent disability their library has. Teachers can share the Anti-Defamation League's guide for Evaluating Children's Books that Address Disability (2013) that provides criteria such as "Avoid books that . . . cast people with disabilities as victims and evoke pity, sorrow, or sentimentality" and "Choose books that . . . promote positive images of persons with disabilities and represent them as strong, independent people" (p. 3). Students can check out the available books in their library, read them, and evaluate them based on these criteria. Then, they can create book trailers for the books they like the most and that are the most affirming toward people with disabilities. They could have a book trailer screening, or maybe share their trailers as a preview to the above-mentioned film activity. Donations gathered could be used to purchase more books that portray characters with disabilities for their school and local libraries.

A Time to Dance offers students a look into various aspects of disability and how it can impact people of all ages. In studying about disability and ways to help reduce or eliminate barriers to access for those with disabilities, students can take one step in creating a more equitable school, community, and world.

SUPPLEMENTAL RESOURCES

Connected Young Adult Literature

Shark Girl by Kelly Bingham
Insignificant Events in the Life of a Cactus by Dusti Bowling
Out of My Mind by Sharon Draper

Connected Short Story Anthologies

Unbroken: 13 Stories Starring Disabled Teens by Marieke Nijkamp
Owning It: Stories about Teens with Disabilities edited by Don Gallo

Connected Music

"Turn! Turn! Turn!" by the Byrds
"Rise Up" by Andra Day
"Scars to Your Beautiful" by Alessia Cara

Connected Films

Finding Nemo
Finding Dory
Soul Surfer
Wonder
Miss You Can Do It

Connected Videos

Girish, R. (2018). Kannaki - Bharatanatyam by 11 year old Sreelakshmi Makreri. https://www.youtube.com/watch?v=87lWe3KyMVE

Niketon, Sri Rama Nataka. (2020). Winner of Angikam International Bharatanatyam Dance Competition - Vanshika Sudarsan. https://www.youtube.com/watch?v=_QYDAmtCRFU

Paralympic Games. (2020). History of the Summer Paralympic Games. https://www.youtube.com/watch?v=xqg4v-BZb1M

Spectrum O&P. (2022). Inspirational Person of the Month Adrianne Haslet-Davis. https://www.spectrumoandp.com/inspirational-person-month-adrianne-haslet-davis/

Tedx Talks (2017). What is Normal? Born Just Right . . . Jordan Reeves. https://www.youtube.com/watch?v=5t7kFRQ5S-4

REFERENCES

Anti-Defamation League. (2013). *Evaluating children's books that address disability*. Education Division. https://www.adl.org/sites/default/files/evaluating-children-s-books-that-address-disability.pdf

Born just right. (n.d.). https://www.bornjustright.org/

Davidson, M. (2006). Universal design: The work of disability in an age of globalization. In L. J. Davis (Ed.), *The disability studies reader* (2nd ed., pp. 117–128). Routledge.

Doctors without borders. (2022). https://www.doctorswithoutborders.org/

Gargiulo, R. M. (2009). *Special education in contemporary society: An introduction to exceptionality* (3rd ed.). Los Angeles, CA: Sage.

HIE Help Center. (2018). Disability awareness class activity lesson plans. https://hiehelpcenter.org/disability-awareness-class-lessons/index.html

International Paralympic Committee. (n.d.). Paralympics history. https://www.paralympic.org/ipc/history

National Youth Leadership Network. (2006). Respectful disability language: Here's what's up! https://www.aucd.org/docs/add/sa_summits/Language%20Doc.pdf

Rozler, L. (2018). Words hurt! https://wordsonalimb.com/2018/11/23/words-hurt/

Society for Disability Studies. (2022). Mission and history. https://disstudies.org/index.php/about-sds/mission-and-history/

The Asia Society. Jati: The caste system in India. (2022). https://asiasociety.org/education/jati-caste-system-india

United Spinal Association. (n.d.). Disability etiquette: Top 10 tips. https://unitedspinal.org/pdf/Disability_Etiquette_Top_10.pdf

United States Census Bureau. (2022). Anniversary of American with Disabilities Act, July 26, 2022: Press Release Number CB22-FF.07. https://www.census.gov/newsroom/facts-for-features/2022/disabilities-act.html

United States Department of Health and Human Services. Centers for Disease Control and Prevention. (n.d.). Disability and health overview. https://www.cdc.gov/ncbddd/disabilityandhealth/disability.html

Vision to Learn (2022). https://visiontolearn.org/

Chapter 8

Black Lives Matter

Racism, particularly anti-Black racism, has plagued many nations across the globe for centuries and in particular the United States. However, in more recent years, national movements have mobilized to combat racism, draw attention to its insidious nature, and work against structural oppression for equity and liberation. One such organization that has become prominent is the Black Lives Matter movement. Their website explains:

> #BlackLivesMatter was founded in 2013 in response to the acquittal of Trayvon Martin's murderer. Black Lives Matter Global Network Foundation, Inc. is a global organization in the US, UK, and Canada, whose mission is to eradicate white supremacy and build local power to intervene in violence inflicted on Black communities by the state and vigilantes. By combating and countering acts of violence, creating space for Black imagination and innovation, and centering Black joy, we are winning immediate improvements in our lives. (Black Lives Matter, n.d., para. 1)

The movement has organized and led massive protests and engaged in meaningful community and solidarity building around the numerous and unjust killings of Black Americans, including Michael Brown, George Floyd, Breonna Taylor, and Ahmaud Arbery as well as supported events such as the nomination of Ketanji Brown Jackson to the Supreme Court. They also provide webinars and host other events to promote education, healing, and justice. Their website further explains:

> Black Lives Matter (BLM) is an ideological and political intervention in a world where Black lives are systematically and intentionally targeted for demise. It is an affirmation of Black folks' humanity, our contributions to this society, and our resilience in the face of deadly oppression. (Black Lives Matter, n.d., para. 3)

The evidence that supports BLM is overwhelming. The *Washington Post* (2022) reports, "Although half of the people shot and killed by police are

White, Black Americans are shot at a disproportionate rate. They account for less than 13 percent of the U.S. population, but are killed by police at more than twice the rate of White Americans" (para. 5). Video footage of unarmed individuals being senselessly murdered also continues to demonstrate the problem. Exacerbating the issue is that, historically, police officers and other instigators have rarely been charged and even more rarely convicted for these instances or have been acquitted. As noted above, the catalyst for BLM was the lack of recourse to prosecute a murderer, and as Dewan (2012), a *New York Times* reporter, notes, "Union protections that shield police officers from timely investigation, legal standards that give them the benefit of the doubt, and a tendency to take officers at their word have added up to few convictions and little prison time for officers who kill" (para. 8).

The role of implicit bias, "a form of bias that occurs automatically and unintentionally, that nevertheless affects judgments, decisions, and behaviors" (National Institute of Health, 2022, para. 2) is at play in the issue of police brutality. Examining implicit bias shifts the focus from individual acts of racism and overt and intentional actions to how negative messages are so deeply ingrained in our socialization through media, cultural practices, and language, that they manifest in actions in more latent ways. As such, a focus on recognizing implicit biases has necessitated a rise in related training and research.

Students will likely be familiar with the concept of implicit bias and with the phrase Black Lives Matter, their flag, and/or their association with political events, yet they may not fully understand why a movement like BLM was necessary in terms of the history that prompted its creation. As instances of police brutality continue to occur and the pervasiveness of racism and implicit bias remains, it is crucial to focus our attention in classrooms particularly on the fact that Black lives indeed matter and to not only illustrate the myriad ways that racism impacts this group but everyone. In this chapter, we draw on the novel *Blended* (Draper, 2018) to illustrate how teachers can talk about these topics and can inspire students to action to disrupt racism in their local contexts as well as on a broader scale.

BLENDED

Sharon Draper's (2018) *Blended* tells the story of Isabella (Izzy), an eleven-year-old dealing with her divorced parents and living between their two homes. Her wealthy lawyer father is Black, while her working-class mother is white. Both are in serious relationships and become engaged to marry their significant others as the novel progresses. Isabella struggles with her biracial identity throughout the novel, experiencing questions about how and who she claims to be. After a heated discussion on lynching in her social studies class, someone leaves a noose in her friend's locker during their PE class. This disturbs the young girls and opens an investigation at school, causing Isabella to further question how she identifies as a child of a Black father and a white mother.

A talented piano player, Izzy practices throughout the chapters for her recital where she will showcase a difficult piece she has learned to play. Her future stepbrother takes her for ice cream on the way to her long-awaited show, and the two are stopped by the police who suspect they were involved in a robbery that has just taken place moments before. Believing Izzy to reach for a weapon when she goes for her cell phone, police shoot and injure the young girl, causing her to not only miss her recital but also to begin a journey of recovery both physically and emotionally. Ultimately, the event brings her disparate family together, and Izzy feels a sense of belonging for the first time.

TEACHING STRATEGIES

Before Reading

As mentioned above, students will likely have heard of the Black Lives Matter movement through the news and social media, but they may not be fully aware of its purpose and origin as well as the variety of responses it has received. Teachers can begin with a web quest that tasks students with exploring the BLM site as well as the history and data that led to its creation. They might examine recent court cases involving police brutality and create a presentation on what happened at the incident and what the outcomes were. During this inquiry, it is crucial to define the term white supremacy and to clear up any misconceptions or misuses of the phrase. Quoting the Challenging White Supremacy Workshop in San Francisco, CA, Martinez (2017) explains: "White supremacy is an historically based, institutionally-perpetuated system of exploitation and oppression of continents, nations, and peoples of color by white peoples and nations of the European continent, for the purpose of maintaining and defending a system of wealth, power, and privilege" (p. 16). Teachers can unpack different portions of this definition such as what it means to be *institutionally* sanctioned (see Chapter 6 on teaching about institutions) and how *privilege* is being used.

The emphasis in this definition is on structures in order to work against the idea that racism is individually enacted and with malicious intent. Martinez (2017) explains that when we refuse to acknowledge the systemic aspect of racism, we demean its effects. This relates to the issue of police brutality,

"Racist police behavior is often reduced to a 'few bad apples' who need to be removed, instead of seeing that it can be found in police departments everywhere." Helping students discern how racism exists in the media (see Chapter 3 on colorism) and is perpetuated through language practices is therefore critical. For example, teachers could have students read Wabuke's (2021) article, "Disney's Disembodied Black Characters," in which the mother writes about her search with her seven-year-old for television or film with Black protagonists. She critiques limited presentations in which even a movie with a Black female lead is featured mostly as an animal and not in her own body. Students could extend this work with their own examples of how Black characters are not the lead or how they are represented, if they are present in film or television.

In addition to an introduction to these concepts, teachers should explore the notion of *microaggressions* with students, as they arise consistently in the novel as well as in students' own lives. Microaggressions are "Brief and commonplace daily verbal, behavioral, and environmental indignities, whether intentional or unintentional, that communicate hostile, derogatory, or negative racial slights and insults to the target person or group" (Sue et al., 2007, p. 273). While this definition focuses on race, microaggressions can be targeted at any marginalized group (e.g., women, people with disabilities). The Pragmatic Mom site has valuable resources and examples of microaggressions for teaching about them with younger children. It suggests using a children's book, *Where Are You From?* (Mendez & Kim, 2019), about a young girl whose peers insist she answer that question despite her uncertainty, to teach about a common microaggression.

This site also includes ways to respond to microaggressions, which is also important to cover with students. Scholarship on *microresistance* would be informative for teachers regarding this topic, as these are "small-scale individual or collaborative efforts that empower targeted people and allies to cope with, respond to, and challenge microaggressions with a goal of disrupting systems of oppression as they unfold in everyday life . . . " (Ganote et al, 2021). Responding with a question, for example, or wearing a quizzical expression in reaction to a microaggression can be a form of microresistance. For example, if a white student tells an Asian-American peer that they must be smart, the teacher can intervene with a question on why that student thinks that, or why people in society often think that. This a potential opportunity for the teacher to help the class unpack where such ideas come from, how they are supported in media and society, and how they keep us from pluralizing our understanding of Asian-Americans (who come from a number of different countries and cultures) and identities, in general. This small act of questioning does not allow for the comment to be taken for granted. Or, if a student says they don't see color and are met with a confused expression by a classmate, this might open the door for a discussion of how we see differences and why. When we provide these options for students, they are better equipped with the tools needed to create change and disrupt problematic statements and actions.

During Reading

The introduction to Black Lives Matter sets the stage for the micro-instances of discrimination in the text and to references to the ways Black individuals are oppressed. These are all worthy of discussion with students, especially how they compound to create a broader system. For example, Isabella's dad, in talking to her about her frayed jeans, tells her "I think it's important we look our very best at all times . . . The world looks at Black people differently. It's not fair, but it's true . . . the world can't see the inside of a person. What the world *can* see is the color" (Draper, 2018, p. 39). Teachers might ask students: *What does Isabella's dad mean about the world being able to see color? What does it mean when people say they are "colorblind," and how does Izzy's dad disagree with this concept? When we see color, then what should we "do" with it?*

Students can extend this discussion into brainstorming a list of ways that "seeing" color has led to problematic actions in the past. Izzy's dad tells her, "Black folks are followed more often than others" (p. 41) in stores. In response, she wonders "if my mom ever thought about this kind of stuff when she shopped" (p. 41), recognizing that her white mother likely had different life experiences than Izzy and others like her. Later in the novel, Izzy and Imani, her best friend who is also Black, are asked to leave a store by a security guard who says, "My job is to remove possible . . . threats." (p. 172). Students could use this to brainstorm a list of the ways that discrimination plays out in both small and big ways. Then they could create another list of ways these actions could be addressed. For example, training security guards on implicit bias would help the issue of being followed in a store. Spreading awareness of "colorblindness" as a negative aspect rather than a positive could enhance appreciation for difference and a more nuanced understanding of people.

Later in the book, Mr. Kazilly asks students in Izzy's class if they know "*why* young people are protesting" at the time of the novel, and Gretchen shares that it is in response to school shootings. He asks if students have the "right to walk out of school" (p. 71). During this section, students can look up the shootings and protests being referred to. Teachers could ask: *Are students allowed to protest at our school? What might happen if they did? What are the pros and cons of a walkout? What rights do students have in schools?* They can research any answers they do not know in small groups and return to share information with the class. Further, when the group in the book talks about how these movements have led to change, Jontay says, " not enough" (p. 73). Teachers can ask: *What does Jontay mean here? What still needs to change in our society, and why? How might those changes be accomplished?*

The reflection on history and making change includes a powerful classroom scene that is pivotal in the book. The teacher asks if students know what *lynching* means, and a discussion ensues. During this, "Logan puts his hands around his neck and fakes like he's choking" (p. 75). His insensitivity causes varied reactions from his classmates and teacher, and Imani strongly reacts, shouting, "Real people were once executed by hanging. With a rope and noose. People like me! That is *not* funny. I'll say it again. *You* are an idiot!" (p. 76). Teachers should take care not to undermine or demean Imani's reaction, but rather to validate it and help students understand her response as warranted. Returning to the idea of microaggressions from before reading, teachers can remind students of "intent versus impact," in such situations. While Logan may not have realized the impact his small gesture would have, it hurt his classmate deeply. He may have considered it a joke, but the reference was to a time in history when such behavior was acceptable and when massive numbers of Black people were slaughtered by the hands of white men. The teacher's response here is, in addition to validating Imani, helping people like Logan understand how they cause harm and how they must be vigilant against such thoughts and moments moving forward.

Later in the novel, a salesperson asks Izzy, "Are you from one of the islands? . . . Or are you mixed?" (p. 168). Izzy plays the question off with a joke, but it clearly bothers her. While the salesperson thought she was complimenting Izzy's beauty, the young girl finds her question offensive. In a final example, Izzy and her mother run into Clint Hammond in the mall and he tells her, "I had no idea your mother was white. That's how you get your good looks, I guess . . . Mixed kids are always pretty" (p. 247). Again, although Clint likely thought he was praising Izzy, his words inflict pain; Izzy calls him out, saying, "If I weren't pretty, then that would have come from my dad?" (p. 247), to which Clint is speechless. Some questions to guide a discussion of these instances are: *Why did the speaker's words (or gestures) hurt the person on the receiving end? What might help Logan, the salesperson, or Clint understand how they caused Izzy to feel bad? How can they show Logan or Clint the broader issues at play in their words?*

Students could journal about a time they have experienced a mismatch in intent versus impact, a time in which they caused unintentional harm. If not comfortable journaling this, they could also choose to write about such an instance they have witnessed or one in the media. Teachers can remind students that microaggressions can occur with regard to race, gender, sexuality, ability, or other systems of oppression, and they might give an example of their own to facilitate students' writing. For example, a teacher who identifies as a woman might share when a male colleague complimented her athletic skills on a co-ed softball team, saying that she threw the ball well for a woman. She might explain how she felt demeaned by what was, according to the speaker, a compliment.

After Logan's action in class, Imani finds a noose in her locker upon returning from gym class. This leads to a school shutdown and an investigation by authorities. Readers learn that Imani's parents are "very active in a racial justice group" (p. 89) and thus there are concerns that her safety may be in jeopardy. Izzy is questioned by authorities as to her involvement and knowledge of the incident, and she is asked what race she puts on "official school forms." She responds: "I'm not sure" (p. 79). Her struggle to navigate her biracial identity is consistent in the novel, and teachers could engage students in considering why it is so difficult for her, asking: *Why does Izzy feel she has to choose to be Black or white? What about society makes us think we need to have an established identity (that fits into boxes)? How do we figure out who we are and how we identify?* Students might write a dialogue in which they give Izzy advice at this point in the text and provide strategies for being comfortable with who she is (see Chapter 3 on self confidence and identity).

After Reading

The novel ends somewhat abruptly after an intense scene in which Izzy and her future stepbrother, Darren, are brutalized by police who suspect they were involved in a robbery. Darren is forced onto the ground with "at least three policeman . . . on top of him" and other officers surround him "with their guns drawn. Aimed at Darren" (p. 267). One, who sees Izzy reaching for her cell phone, then shoots and injures her arm, causing her to fall and resulting in a serious concussion. Izzy recovers in the hospital, surrounded by her entire family, who work to get along on her behalf and pray together for her well-being. Izzy shares that in response, "Activists are screaming. Police brutality. Child endangerment. And apparently, Black Lives Matter has put me at the top of its list! I think about that one for a minute" (p. 300). Unpacking what happened with students and making connections back to Black Lives Matter to bring the unit full circle is crucial. Teachers can ask: *How could this situation have been deescalated instead of going the way it did? Although this is a work of fiction, what other instances from BLM did you hear about that are similar? What happened in those cases? How could the police have responded differently? How did implicit bias play a role in their responses?*

In addition to this aspect, teachers could focus on the characters' racial battle fatigue and post-traumatic stress after reading. Izzy's friend Imani suffers after the noose incident, but readers only get small glimpses into her pain. For example, one night while having a slumber party, the girls come across a movie for which the advertisement includes a "cowboy with a flat-brimmed hat, scowling like he's really angry. He's looking directly at a noose, which fills the screen" (p. 132). Imani shakes and after her mother helps calm her down, she admits to her friends that sometimes she has nightmares. After Darren and Izzy experience their encounter with the police, Darren tells Izzy, "I gotta admit—I'm still pretty freaked out . . . I feel like there's somebody behind me. Kinda . . . [ellipses in original] jumpy, y'know" (p. 286).

Students could consider the effects of these incidents on the characters and those around them, noting what other consequences they may be experiencing (see Chapter 1 for teaching about trauma). They might research post-traumatic stress disorder and discuss how Imani, Izzy, and Darren may be suffering similar symptoms. Relatedly, teachers could read about racial trauma with students through, for example, Mental Health America's (2022) site, which includes information on "direct" and "vicarious" traumatic stressors. Teachers can ask students: *How were Imani, Darren, and Izzy's experiences a direct encounter? Where in the novel were vicarious experiences? What suggestions could you provide for each of them to begin to heal from the incidents? What might the school have done in the noose situation to ensure more safety and education for* ALL *of the students? What do you think of the way the school handled the situation? What should the police have done following the situation with Darren and Izzy?*

In addition to exploring these aspects related to racism in the book, students can also engage with the ways stereotypes are disrupted. They could create a list, for example, of how the book addresses stereotypes. For instance, Izzy's father is very involved in her life, defying the stereotype that Black men are not attentive fathers. Furthermore, her white mother is working class, while her father is upper class, defying additional stereotypes about race and wealth. Her stepbrother is a fashionable, driven Black man, again defying stereotypes about Black youth and their interests. Once they have these lists, they could also determine what could be done to take action to address these stereotypes or how they can move themselves beyond them. Teachers could also draw from activities outlined by Jewell (2020) in *This Book is Anti-racist*, such as creating their own identity maps and understanding their social identities. They might find exploring the publisher's website (Simon & Schuster, 2022), especially the author's interview videos, illuminating. Draper shares that the incident of police brutality was in fact based on real events that happened in her family.

INTERSECTIONS

This book focuses largely on racism and Izzy's identity as a biracial young woman. However, there are several intersections with additional areas that would allow for more in depth teaching and text-to-self connections for readers. The most prominent is that of family dynamics, as Izzy is constantly moving between her mother's and father's homes, which contain different expectations, norms, and challenges. She describes the tension amongst her parents at the weekly "exchange day" at the mall, and she recounts how they fight at different times in the book over their shared custody. For instance, at one point, Izzy's mother is intentionally late to meet her father, and he calls the police. Izzy is devastated and runs away. Even though her father feels badly for his mistake, he later explains, "Custody is a delicate dance, sweetie. Each side has to comply, or the judge can change the agreement" (p. 143). At another time, Izzy's father schedules his wedding on the same day as her mother's and on her mother's day of custody, which becomes a glaring issue.

The trials of being a child of divorce are common to many students, and teachers could ask them to empathize with Izzy and create a T chart of how her mom's and dad's houses are different. Then, they could use this to connect to Izzy's struggle with identity and note why it is that Izzy might feel as conflicted as she does about who she is. They could research statistics on divorce (and custody) to note aspects such as its prevalence in the United States. They might also create lists of the positives and negatives of living in two places so as to show that there are some possible advantages to such situations (e.g., having two loving families).

In addition to family dynamics, the book highlights differences in social class. As referenced above, Izzy's dad, a lawyer, is financially secure and her mother, a waitress at Waffle House, has more limited income. Her father takes her to nice restaurants, has a home with a piano, and purchases her nice clothes. Her mother works hard, takes her bowling where her boyfriend is the manager, and has a Casio keyboard for Izzy to practice on in her bedroom. Izzy seems happy in both homes and likes both of her parents' finances, which could lead to a discussion with students on what is needed for children to feel safe and loved. Students could create visuals of what Izzy likes about each of her homes. They could then share, via post-it notes on the board, what they would like to have in their own dream homes. They could then categorize those into themes of which are similar and different, recognizing how those overlap and diverge for individuals.

SOCIAL ACTION PROJECTS

Extending the pre-, during-, and after-reading activities into social action projects is crucial. Building from their knowledge of BLM, students might write to the organization in support. Regarding microaggressions and microresistance, they might keep a log for one week of microaggressions they see, hear, or even experience and then, with a partner, create strategies for responding to those specific ones. For example, if they overhear someone at school using gender references as an insult (e.g., "He's such a girl, he is into gossip") they might respond with a question ("what does that even mean, he's a girl?," a statement, "that's not cool, saying all girls gossip," or a gesture, like an eye roll or a shrug) to show that they are resisting the language of the perpetrator. Furthermore, students could extend their brainstorming from the during-reading strategies to how seeing color has produced problematic actions in the past and then act on their resolutions, such as spreading awareness of colorblindness as a misguided concept or advocating for more training of school staff on implicit bias.

In class, Izzy and her peers consider a way to respond to the noose incident, to take action in a positive way. During the discussion, Izzy says, " I think the only thing that gets rid of hate is love" (p. 101) and they decide to hang hearts all over the school that say things like "HONOR OUR DIFFERENCES," "ALL YOU NEED IS LOVE," and "HATE-FREE ZONE" (p. 139). Students could imitate this action with their own symbol of positivity, such as a heart, a school mascot, or a peace sign and they could post sayings along with the object to encourage unity. They could ask other classes and clubs to join the effort so that it is school-wide and represents different groups and grade levels. They could then create an anonymous wall where students could post ways they have translated these sayings into action with students reporting their actions.

Throughout the novel, Heather, Izzy's friend who is white, is an ally to Izzy and Imani. After the noose incident, Heather says, "I feel guilty, like . . . it's my fault, because it was probably somebody white who put the noose in her locker" (p. 102) and later when she learns about her friends being kicked out of the store in the mall she says, "But . . . but . . . Somebody's got to *do* something!" (p. 175). Students, relating to Heather's desperate need for action, could research and create materials on how to be an ally to friends of color. As inspiration, they could watch a video in which Bettina Love (2019) explain the story of a white man who used his privilege to support a Black woman climbing a pole to remove a confederate flag. Or, they could examine the University of Colorado at Boulder's website (2020) with lists of ways to become a better ally to Black communities. They might anonymously survey and listen to students of color in their school (careful not to make one student a spokesperson, however) and use this as input for their posters or PSAs. Such a project would bring students together and encourage them to engage in authentic dialogue.

Finally, students could join local movements, protests, or marches or develop their own at their school in their community. They might make t-shirts to support the cause or host an informative event at their school. They could research local policies on officer training and suggest additional measures as needed. As a whole, *Blended* provokes youth to not only consider the historic ways racism has played a part in their country's history but also to address the ways it is still present today, and it provides multiple avenues for doing so.

SUPPLEMENTAL RESOURCES

Connected Young Adult Literature

A Good Kind of Trouble by Lisa Moore Ramée
One Crazy Summer by Rita Williams-Garcia
Betty Before X by Ilyasah Shabazz and Renée Watson
March by John Lewis and Andrew Aydin

Connected Music

"Black Like Me" by Mickey Guyton
"Young, Gifted and Black" by Nina Simone
"Freedom" by Beyoncé (feat. Kendrick Lamar)

Connected Poetry

"A Small Needful Fact" by Ross Gay
"Fury and Faith" by Amanda Gorman
"not an elegy for Mike Brown" by Danez Smith

REFERENCES

Black Lives Matter. (n.d.). About. https://blacklivesmatter.com/about/
Black Lives Matter. (n.d.). Herstory. https://blacklivesmatter.com/herstory/
Dewan, S. (2020, September 24). Few police officers who cause deaths are charged or convicted. *The New York Times*. https://www.nytimes.com/2020/09/24/us/police-killings-prosecution-charges.html

Draper, S. (2018). *Blended*. Atheneum Books for Young Readers.
Fatal force. (2022). *The Washington Post*. https://www.washingtonpost.com/graphics/investigations/police-shootings-database/
Ganote, C., Souza, T., & Cheung, F. (2021). Pedagogies of microresistance for equity and social justice. In R. Kumar & B. Refaei (eds.), Equity and inclusion in higher education, Chapter 5. https://ucincinnatipress.manifoldapp.org/read/chapter-5-pedagogies-of-microresistance-for-equity-and-social-justice/section/6f46153b-0ed2-40df-80b0-ad2d8aa8f96f
Jewell, T. & Durand, A. (Illustrator). (2020). *This book is anti-racist*. Frances Lincoln Children's Books.
Love, B. (2019). User clip: Dr. Bettina Love explains what she means by a co-conspirator. C-Span. https://www.c-span.org/video/?c4880307/user-clip-dr-bettina-love-explains-means-conspirator
Martinez, E. B. (2017). What is white supremacy? *Catalyst project*. https://www.pym.org/annual-sessions/wp-content/uploads/sites/7/2017/06/What_Is_White_Supremacy_Martinez.pdf
Méndez, Y. S. & Kim, J. (2019). *Where are you from?* HarperCollins.
Mental Health America. (2022). Racial trauma. https://www.mhanational.org/racial-trauma
National Institute of Health. (2022). Implicit bias. https://diversity.nih.gov/sociocultural-factors/implicit-bias.
Pragmatic Mom. (2020, June). A unit to teach kids about microaggressions. https://www.pragmaticmom.com/2020/06/teach-kids-about-microaggressions/
Simon & Schuster. The book pantry: Featured author, Sharon Draper. https://simonandschusterpublishing.com/thebookpantry/aotm-sharon-draper.html
Sue, D. W., Capodilupo, C. M., Torino, G. C., Bucceri, J. M., Holder, A. M. B., Nadal, K., L., & Esquilin, M. (2007). Racial microaggressions in everyday life: implications for clinical practice. *American Psychologist, 62*(4), 271–286.
University of Colorado. (2020). How to be an ally to the Black community and communities of color. https://www.colorado.edu/today/2020/06/03/how-be-ally-black-community-and-communities-color
Wabuke, H. (2021, March 23). Disney's disembodied black characters. *Los Angeles Review of Books*. https://lareviewofbooks.org/article/disneys-disembodied-black-characters/

Chapter 9

Foster Care And Stigma

According to the Annie E. Casey Foundation, foster care is "a temporary living situation for children whose parents cannot take care of them. While in care, children may live with relatives, with foster families or in group facilities" (para. 2). In 2020, more than 407,000 children were in foster care, a total number that has been decreasing since 2017. Children can leave foster care in four ways: "reunification with birth parents or primary caregivers, adoption, guardianship, and placement with relatives. Among children exiting foster care each year, nearly half—more than 107,000 kids in 2020—are reunited with a parent or primary caretaker" (The Annie E. Casey Foundation, 2022, para. 2). Due to stigmas surrounding being part of the foster care system, pre-teens and teens may be unfamiliar with the system in general and the social justice issues connected to being in foster care. Searches for teaching resources regarding how to teach about foster care yield limited results beyond trauma-sensitive teaching strategies to support students in foster care, a fact that makes it feel even more important to spend classroom time on this topic. In this chapter, we offer teachers and students ways to learn more about myths and stereotypes regarding foster care families as well as ideas for developing social action projects connected to supporting those in the foster system. Jacqueline Woodson's (2003) novel in verse *Locomotion* will serve as the focal text for a unit of study connected to foster care.

LOCOMOTION

Jacqueline Woodson's (2003) novel, *Locomotion*, is written in verse format. The protagonist, Lonnie Collins Motion (Lo Co Motion), has written a series of poems that help the reader gain a glimpse into his life. Lonnie is in foster care, living with "Miss Edna," after his parents were killed in a fire. His sister, Lili, has been placed with a different foster family that wants to adopt her. Lonnie's teacher, Ms. Marcus, has the students in her class keep poetry notebooks, and readers get to see what Lonnie has written for each poetry assignment in addition to the poems he writes on his own time. Through his poems, written in a variety of formats such as haiku, sonnet, epistle, list, and epitaph, readers learn about Lonnie's wonderings, memories, trauma, and healing as a child growing up in foster care.

TEACHING STRATEGIES

Before Reading

Before reading *Locomotion*, teachers might want to introduce some general information regarding what foster care is and what it is not, the history of foster care in the United States, and terminology connected with foster care. It will be important for teachers not to reinforce negative stereotypes about families needing to use foster care, foster parents, and children receiving foster care. Sites like the National Foster Parent Association and the Court Appointed Special Advocates provide timelines with basic historical information regarding foster care and its progression throughout history. In learning about the history of foster care, students might want to do some additional research on topics like the Children's Aid Society, the Orphan Trains of the mid-1800s, or the more recent Adoption and Safe Families Act.

Terms like foster care, foster system, foster families, and group home can be defined with examples. The Child Welfare Information Gateway provides an extensive glossary from which teachers can select vocabulary words, or, perhaps, have individual students choose their own five to ten terms to learn about and share with the rest of the class. After terms are reviewed, teachers might engage students in a myth-busters activity, using, for example, the carousel graffiti method, writing some statements about foster care either on large chart paper, or spread out on white/chalkboards. Students can start at different statements around the room, silently reading and then writing or drawing their thoughts/reactions to what they read, identifying whether or not they believe the statement is true and then sharing their personal response. After a few minutes, teachers can have students rotate, moving on to the next statement and doing the same. Once students have responded to all of the prompts, teachers can share the myth buster information with them (see chart below for some examples of statements and explanations).

Following this activity, teachers might ask students questions like: *What surprised you? What did you learn from this information? What might you already have known?* They might extend the conversation by asking students some guiding questions such as: *When might a family need to use foster care? What are the benefits of foster care? What might be some difficulties of being*

Table 9.1.

Statement about foster care	Facts
The majority of children in the foster care system have been abused.	The reality is that only 17% of children who enter foster care are in the system because they have been abused (Roberts, 2022, para. 3).
Children can be put into foster care because their family lacks food, housing, and/or clothing.	Most of the children in foster care are placed there because of "neglect"—lack of food, housing, and/or clothing (Roberts, 2022, para. 3).
Very few (less than 5%) of children in the United States are part of an investigation by Child Protective Services before their eighteenth birthday.	More than a third (37.4%) of all children in the United States have experienced a CPS investigation by the time they are eighteen years old.
Parental alcohol abuse is a leading factor in children being placed in foster care.	In 2019, alcohol abuse played a role in 5% of child removals (Children's Defense Fund, 2022, para. 4).
The goal of foster care is to get adopted.	Foster care is meant to be temporary. The goal of foster care is reunification with the family, not adoption (Children's Defense Fund, 2022, para. 9).
The majority of children in foster care are teenagers.	In 2019, 41% of children in foster care were under the age of six (Children's Defense Fund, 2022, para. 5). Kids one to five years old made up 30% of all children placed in foster care in 2020, and 7% were babies (Annie E. Casey, 2022, para. 7).
Black children are almost twice as likely to be part of a CPS investigation as white children.	"More than half of Black children are subjected to a CPS investigation at some point during their childhoods—almost twice the lifetime prevalence for White children" (Roberts, 2022, para. 6).
One-third of teenagers in foster care are in a congregate (group home, residential treatment center, hospital) placement.	"In 2017, a third of teenagers in foster care were in a congregate setting" (Roberts, 2022, para. 8).

placed in foster care? What are some positives of being placed in foster care? What are some emotions people in foster care might feel and why? Teachers can then share some of the statistics regarding foster care, such as its prevalence. In 2020, three out of 1,000 children a year (213,964) were placed in foster care, and 34% of children were placed with family members in 2020 (Annie E. Casey, 2022, para. 11). In 2020, 48% of children returned to their home families after time in foster care (Annie E. Casey, 2022, para. 21).

Teachers can ask students: *Were any of these statistics different from what you expected? Why or why not?* They can press students to try to identify where their information/ideas regarding foster care have come from. In tracking students' thoughts and beliefs, they can, if warranted, help to dispel myths as well as take the time to discuss the importance of finding credible sources for information as well as questioning depictions seen on television and in film. If all examples students come up with are negative, teachers can ask questions like: *What are the dangers in relying on depictions in film or television? Why do you think producers create films with negative portrayals of families?*

Teachers might also want to review or introduce what a novel in verse is, in case students are new to the format. Teachers can lead students in sharing what they think a novel in verse is and what they think are the advantages and drawbacks of this format for readers. Teachers might also introduce/review different poetry terms with students. There are a multitude of websites that provide lists of poetry terms that teachers can use, such as Scholastic's Poetry Terms to Know: A Quick Refresher (2022). A list could be posted somewhere in the classroom, and then students could refer to it as they read the novel, identifying the poetry terms as they find them.

During Reading

This novel lends itself to combination with a unit of study on poetry. As students read the different chapters, they can analyze the poems Lonnie has written, referring to their poetry terms and identifying types of poems and characteristics within the poems they read. Further, they can use Lonnie's poems as inspiration and models to write their own poems for their personal poetry notebooks. For example, there are multiple forms of poems that Lonnie writes, including haiku, sonnet, epistle poem, list poem, occasional poem, and epitaph poem. As students identify Lonnie's poems in the various formats, teachers can guide students in reading other poems in those formats and then in writing their own poems. At the end of the unit, students can share their favorite poems they have written with the class, the school, or the community.

Opportunities for writing in formats other than poetry present themselves through reading the novel as well. Often when Locomotion talks about his mother, he mentions how she smelled, like honeysuckle and talcum powder. Teachers can use this poem as an introduction to writing a descriptive essay that connects a scent with a memory. The poem "Describe Somebody" (pp. 22–23) offers another writing prompt where students, like Lonnie, could "Take out your poetry notebooks and describe somebody" (p. 22), later turning this poem into a larger descriptive essay.

The poem "Group Home Before Miss Edna's House" provides opportunities for students to further investigate group homes. Lonnie says the boys with whom he lives at the group home call themselves "The Throwaway Boys" (p. 15) and that on "one rainy Saturday afternoon while you're sitting at the Group Home window reading a beat-up Group Home book, wearing a Group Home hand-me-down shirt hearing all the Group Home loudness" (p. 16) it occurs to him that he, too, is a "Throwaway Boy." Teachers might want to lead a discussion having students identify what a "throwaway boy" might mean, and why Lonnie might call himself that. Following, teachers might lead students in discussing the importance of acknowledging their unique and wonderful selves, and not giving in to negative self-esteem. Activities like those in Chapter 3 of this book would fit well here, guiding students to identify the unique qualities they and their classmates have and celebrating those in a public space.

The poem in *Locomotion* "December 9" provides the reader with some insight regarding the trauma Lonnie and his family faced that resulted in his foster care placement. Teachers might want to refer to Chapter 1 and engage students in some of the activities described to help reduce trauma, like deep breathing activities and participation in arts-based activities like drawing, painting, dancing, and writing poetry. This would be an opportune time to help students recognize that writing poems is a positive outlet for Lonnie to release his emotions, share his feelings in a private way, and process his grief. Teachers can help students identify their own personal coping strategies that they can turn to in times of discomfort and stress.

After Reading

The poem "Epistle Poem" references the poet Langston Hughes, and teachers might want to introduce Hughes's poetry to the class as well. After reading and discussing several of Langston Hughes's poems, they might search for other poets and create their own poetry scrapbooks, collecting poems they like, and organizing them by theme. They can keep these poetry books for themselves, give them as a gift to someone they care about, or perhaps consider donating them to a hospital or doctor's waiting room, a nursing home, or a senior center in their community.

The novel offers opportunities for a variety of research, too. Lonnie shares that "Lili's new mama didn't want no boys. Just a sweet little girl. Nobody told me that, I just know it. Not a lot of people want boys. Not foster boys that ain't babies" (p. 46). Teachers might suggest that students conduct research to see if this is true—if girls and babies are more likely to be fostered by families, and if boys are more likely to be placed in group homes. This could also be an opportunity for students to investigate the Indian Child Welfare Act and to make connections between the systems and laws regarding foster families on and off reservations (see Chapter 5). NPR published a series of articles called "Native Foster Care: Lost Children, Shattered Families" that can provide a place to start in learning more about the federal law and the ways in which it historically has and hasn't been upheld (see resources list below).

Searches for songs connected to foster care largely result in lists for foster parents, such as "Five songs every foster parent must hear," "Forty-plus songs for adoption and foster care," and "Songs for foster parents." There are some connected to foster care (see below), but they focus on negative statistics surrounding children who are in foster care. As such, we recommend that teachers work with students to create their own playlists. They could first brainstorm the types of music they would like to include on their playlist with a rationale explaining why. Then they can create the list and add a title. For example, Lonnie likes rap and hip hop, so perhaps students would want to make a playlist with songs from this genre, identifying why they think Lonnie would enjoy them. Similarly, they might create a list for Lonnie's sister Lili. Alternatively, they might choose to create a list for a general audience of children in foster care, including songs that might help make listeners feel peace and joy.

Similarly, the "Happiness Poem" depicts Miss Edna dancing and singing along with the radio. Teachers might lead students in identifying their own sources of happiness. They might ask students: *What songs make you happy? What about those makes you feel joy?* Then students can create their own happiness playlists that they can listen to when they need to be cheered up and/or share with their classmates. To continue with an exploration of music, students might focus on the poem "How I Got My Name" (p. 21), which references the song and dance "The Locomotion." Teachers might want to share the song "Locomotion" and its many iterations with students (see resources list below). Teachers might play different versions of the song and have students identify which version they like best and why. This will open up opportunities to talk about tone and style and how these can impact a work be it written or audio. Students can also discuss which version they think best connects with the character Lonnie in the novel and discuss why they feel that way. They could create position statements on their choices and deliver them to the class, even then engaging in a debate to defend their choice.

INTERSECTIONS

Locomotion has intersections with issues connected to race, poverty, trauma, and bullying, among others. Lonnie and his little sister Lili are Black, and intersections with race are present. For example, in his poem "Mama," Locomotion writes, "I go to the drugstore and before the guard starts following me around like I'm gonna steal something I go to the cosmetics lady and ask her if she has it . . . *No*, I say to the cosmetics lady. *It's not the right one. And then I leave fast. Before somebody asks to check my pockets which are always empty 'cause I don't steal"* (pp. 7–8). Teachers can ask students: *Why might the guard follow Locomotion around? Have you experienced extra surveillance based on your appearance (age, race, gender identification, way you dress, etc.)? How did it make you feel? Why do you think that happens? What do you think can be done to help certain groups not be targeted?*

The poem titled "Commercial Break" (pp. 12–13) demonstrates how Lonnie is seeing connections between race and income. Lonnie has written about a commercial on television that depicts a "white lady making a nice dinner for her husband" (p. 12). His teacher "wants to know why I wrote that the lady is white and I say because it's true." And Ms. Marcus says: *Lonnie, what does race have to do with it* (p. 12). Lonnie goes on to say that Ms. Marcus just:

> don't understand some things . . . Things like my brown, brown arm. And the white lady and man with all that good food to throw away. How if you turn on your TV, that's what you see—people with lots and lots of stuff not having to sit on scratchy couches . . . And the true fact is alotta those people are white. Maybe it's that if you're white you can't see all the whiteness around you. (p. 13)

Later, in the poem "Lamont," Ms. Marcus asks the class, "Do you think poor people aren't happy?" (p. 69). Angel responds, "I don't know. Don't know any poor people. But when you see those pictures on TV of those kids who they want you to send money to, they don't look happy to me, they just look hungry and sad" (p. 69).

Teachers can ask students if they think it is true that commercials tend to depict financially stable white, able-bodied people, and when "poor people" are represented they look hungry and sad. Then they can turn on the television and watch commercials together as a class (or for homework), tracking the diversity they see or don't see and how specific products are displayed. After tracking commercials together, the teacher might ask: *What did you see? What did you NOT see? Why do you think that is? Why is it important? What messages are being sent to consumers through these (lack of) depictions? Have you ever noticed this before?*

Finally, the poem "New Boy" shares specific examples of bullying that Lonnie's new classmate, Clyde, experiences. "Lamont whispers *He should be sorry he's so country.* Eric says *Look at his country clothes*" (p. 29). Teachers can lead students in discussions regarding bullying (see Chapter 3), including questions like: *Why do you think people bully others? Why are we afraid of/ threatened by difference? What are the positives of living in different geographic locales?*

IDEAS FOR SOCIAL ACTION

There are a multitude of opportunities for social action projects connected to foster care, and in all cases teachers should guide students in following their own ideas regarding what they would like to pursue. If they need some suggestions, however, teachers can return to the text and specific poems as a source of inspiration. For example, one of the poems Lonnie writes focuses on group homes, and this might inspire students to do some research to see if group homes exist in their own communities. Lonnie mentions reading a "beat-up Group Home book" and wearing a "Group Home hand-me-down shirt" (p. 16). Students might be inspired to find out what residents in group homes might need and, perhaps more importantly, brainstorm what group home residents might *want*, considering what they might want, if they were in that living situation. Then students could organize a fundraiser or donation drive to raise money/collect those items to be given to the group home members.

In the poem "Visiting," Lonnie describes the "Agency" where he is able to visit with his little sister Lili as "a gray building. It's ugly. It smells like Ajax. The floors got scuffs on them but they shine. There's only a couple windows though and not a whole lot of light coming in" (p. 44). Students might want to do some research and see if such a visiting agency exists in their town. If it does, they may want to schedule a visit to learn more about it and to describe what it looks like inside and out, comparing it to the Agency where Lonnie and Lili visit and speculating why this might be. If their descriptions are similar, students may want to brainstorm ways in which they can help beautify the space, be it painting a mural, bringing in flowers or candles or lamps, or other comforting and lighting options, for example. They can focus on ways to make the space one that inspires joy instead of one that is ugly and dark, if it happens to be that way.

While this exercise is not centered on the topic of foster care, students might want to focus on the experiences of Lonnie's classmate, Eric, who has sickle cell anemia. Eric and Lonnie's teacher, Ms. Marcus, explains to the class what sickle cell is, its symptoms, and treatment and management options. She suggests that the class make Eric a card to cheer him up during his hospital stay. This might inspire students to create cards that can be distributed to their local children's hospital (or children's ward of their local hospital). Students might also investigate what play options are available for hospitalized children and/or their siblings who might have to also spend long days in the hospital with their families. They might collect donations to purchase items like games and books or new soft toys and blankets to be distributed to children and families who have chronic illnesses requiring long hospital stays.

As the novel is written in verse, a clear connection would be to have students write their own poetry. They could then plan a poetry night at a local coffee shop. Students could read their poems and charge admission or collect donations at the door that can later be donated to a cause of their choice or be used to help fund one of the other proposed social action projects mentioned above.

In studying the statistics around foster care, combating myths regarding foster care, and encouraging students to create social action projects connected to supporting those in the foster system, students can take steps to educate themselves and others about this prevalent social justice issue that directly affects their same-age peers in their communities and around the nation.

SUPPLEMENTAL RESOURCES

Connected Young Adult Literature

Far from the Tree by Robin Benway
Forever, or a Long Long Time by Caela Carter
Pictures of Hollis Woods by Patricia Reilly Giff
One for the Murpheys by Lynda Mullaly Hunt
Planet Earth Is Blue by Nicole Panteleakos

Connected Music

"Loco-motion" (1962) by Little Eva
"Loco-motion" (1964) by Pat Boone
"Loco-motion" (1974) by Grand Funk Railroad
"Locomotion" (1980) by Carole King
"Locomotion" (1985) by Raymen
"Loco-motion" (1987) by Kylie Minogue
"Loco-motion" (1988) by Ike and Tina Turner
"Locomotion" (1994) by Charly Garcia
"Loco-motion" (2004) by Dwight Yoakam

Connected Articles

NPR. (2022). Native Foster Care: Lost Children, Shattered Families. https://www.npr.org/series/141763531/native-foster-care-lost-children-shattered-families

National Foster Parent Association. (2020). History of Foster Care in the United States. https://nfpaonline.org/page-1105741

Sethi, A. (2021). A Brief History of Foster Care in the United States. CASA: Court appointed special advocates. https://www.casatravis.org/a_brief_history_of_foster_care_in_the_united_states

Connected Poetry

Power Poems: https://powerpoetry.org/tags/foster-care

Connected Resources on "Ways to Help"

DeGarmo, J. (2021). 10 Ways to Help Children in Foster Care without Being a Foster Parent. https://drjohndegarmo.medium.com/10-ways-to-help-children-in-foster-care-without-being-a-foster-parent-584735a9965a

U.S. Department of Education. (2016). Foster Care Transition Toolkit. https://www2.ed.gov/about/inits/ed/foster-care/youth-transition-toolkit.pdf

REFERENCES

Annie E. Casey Foundation (2022). Foster care. https://www.aecf.org/topics/foster-care Child Welfare Information Gateway. (n.d.). Glossary. https://www.childwelfare.gov/glossary/glossarya/

Children's Defense Fund. (2022). The state of America's children 2021: Child welfare. https://www.childrensdefense.org/state-of-americas-children/soac-2021-child-welfare/

DeGarmo, J. (2021).10 ways to help children in foster care without being a foster parent https://drjohndegarmo.medium.com/10-ways-to-help-children-in-foster-care-without-being-a-foster-parent-584735a9965a

National Foster Parent Association. (2020). History of foster care in the United States. https://nfpaonline.org/page-1105741

NPR. (2022). Native foster care: Lost children, shattered families. https://www.npr.org/series/141763531/native-foster-care-lost-children-shattered-families

Roberts, D. (2022). Five myths about the child welfare system. *The Washington Post.* https://www.washingtonpost.com/outlook/2022/04/15/five-myths-child-welfare/

Scholastic. (2022). Poetry terms to know: A quick refresher. https://www.scholastic.com/parents/books-and-reading/raise-a-reader-blog/poetry-terms-to-know-quick-refresher.html

Sethi, A. (2021). A brief history of foster care in the United States. CASA: Court appointed special advocates. https://www.casatravis.org/a_brief_history_of_foster_care_in_the_united_states

Chapter 10

Experiences of Immigrants

The United States has a fraught history with immigration. Originally taken over in the 1600s by immigrants seeking religious freedom, this country now has more immigrants than any other in the world (Budiman, 2020). In the 1850s, anti-immigrant sentiment grew due to an influx of Irish and Asian populations. Despite the fact that people were fleeing from China due to "war, persecution, and famine" (Washington State Historical Society, 2022, para. 2), Americans felt they were taking potential jobs and therefore pushed for the Chinese Exclusion Act of 1882, banning new immigrants from entering the country for a decade. In the years that followed, federal Immigration Acts "increased the number of inadmissible classes of immigrants, expanded the power of deportation, and raised the head tax on immigrants to $4." Over time, disagreements raged over race-based exclusions and policies favored immigration from certain parts of Europe.

Years later, "In 1965, though, a combination of political, social and geopolitical factors led to passage of the landmark Immigration and Nationality Act that created a new system favoring family reunification and skilled immigrants, rather than country quotas. The law also imposed the first limits on immigration from the Western Hemisphere," (Cohn, 2015, para. 7) particularly those from Latin America. The 2000s saw a heightened response to immigration based on alleged safety concerns, and sanctions for employers who hired undocumented workers were solidified. During these years, former President Obama "took executive action to allow young adults who had been brought to the country illegally to apply for deportation relief and a work permit" (para. 9). Following this, however, former President Trump made sweeping changes to immigration, specifically tightening the US-Mexico border and making it more difficult to immigrate with authorization (Bolter, Israel, & Pierce, 2022).

The reasons that people choose to leave their home countries and come to the United States include "employment opportunities, to escape a violent conflict, environmental factors, educational purposes, or to reunite with family" (National Geographic, 2022, para. 1). Despite the promises of the American Dream, it is actually often a very difficult and complicated path for newcomers to resettle and achieve citizenship. Stories like Enrique's, an eleven-year-old Honduran boy who attempted to reunite with his mother in the United States by riding atop trains through Latin America and braving dangerous conditions, are common (Nazario, 2014). And, once they arrive, immigrants are often treated poorly; Pottinga (2019), for example, tells of how as a child she was asked to step in as a translator for her German mother and remembers a grocery store clerk asking them, "Why don't you go back to where you came from?" (para. 1).

Negative messages about immigrants are rampant in the media and public discourse, although their actual experiences are often much less widespread. Youth therefore are often unfamiliar with facts about immigration, yet they hear misconceptions, stereotypes, and inaccurate information daily. The narrative of choice surrounds immigration when in reality situations are complicated by financial decisions and safety concerns at home. Obtaining citizenship requires time, money, and an interview that contains an English and Civics test (U.S. Citizenship and Immigration Services, 2022). Given that much of the immigrant experience is nebulous to many—but at the same time youth in classrooms may also be immigrants or have parents who are (and may be bullied or stereotyped because of that)—it is imperative that teachers work to represent and unpack immigration with middle-level readers. In this chapter, we hope to help students understand the tumultuous history and status of immigration in the United States through the first person narrative in the novel *Front Desk* (Yang, 2018).

FRONT DESK

In *Front Desk* (Yang, 2018), based on the author Kelly Yang's own experiences, Mia, a ten-year-old Asian girl helps her parents, who immigrated from China, run a motel. Desperate for work, they eagerly accept the position because it includes boarding. However, they quickly learn that the hotel owner, Mr. Yao, exploits them at every turn, making them pay for anything that breaks in the motel as well as for refunds for customers and unreturned keys. Mia befriends "the weeklies," or those who rent at the hotel by the week and live there. At school, she struggles with being bullied for her clothing and her ethnicity, and she has an especially contentious relationship with the motel owner's son, Jason, who wishes to distance himself from Mia publicly but then secretly admits he likes her.

Mia's life is not all gloomy, however. She befriends Lupe, whose father is a handyman for the motel owner and who came with her parents to the

United States from Mexico when she was three years old. They develop a deep friendship and understanding of one another. Throughout the novel, Mia's parents offer free lodging to other immigrants who need a short-term place to stay, and she hears their stories with compassion, seeing how her family treats others as family even when they are not blood related. Hank and the other weeklies turn out to be good friends of hers and they celebrate holidays together. Despite their little means, her parents do their best to give Mia a loving home, and her father purchases her an expensive pencil one day to reassure Mia of her worth after her mother has disparaged her. In the end, Mia leads a successful campaign to purchase the motel with a multitude of investors who grant large and small sums, and she vows to run it humanely with her parents.

TEACHING STRATEGIES

Before Reading

As with the other chapters in this novel, we encourage teachers to begin by defining key concepts related to immigration. Students should understand the difference between an *immigrant*, *refugee*, and a *displaced person* (see Chapter 4 on refugees). They should also gain some familiarity with the history of immigration policy in the United States. Teachers could provide students with particular dates, such as 1882 and 2017 to help scaffold their timelines, or require ten events at least a decade apart, to ensure that students explore the long history of policies and how they shifted over time, particularly how they shifted from targeting Europeans, Asians, and Latin Americans.

To understand contemporary immigration policies, students might watch John Green's YouTube video, "Understanding Trump's Executive Order on Immigration" (Vlogbrothers, 2017), which is part of his Vlogbrothers series in which he creates accessible videos for youth on social topics. Students could also research information about immigrants in the United States, such as the greatest population's country of origin and where most reside in this country. The Pew Research Center (Budiman, 2020) is a great place for students to begin, and a lesson on using publications could accompany this topic and research. *Education World* has some solid ideas for teaching students about credible resources (Lambert, 2022). Once they feel they have enough data, they could create infographics to illustrate their findings, and they could share with classmates what they found, what was surprising from their research, and what they would still like to know. This could guide further research and filter into social action projects later in the unit (see below).

Students should also investigate what happens when a person arrives in the United States from another country and what steps they must take to become citizens. They could find information about the citizenship test and interview as well as examine the complicated fees associated with applying. They might actually take the citizenship test and see how they perform. In addition, teachers might invite local offices who are involved in these processes to speak with students to help them better understand the complicated steps involved. Of course, teachers should never ask students what their status is nor ask them to share with others anything about their family or their own backgrounds.

Specific to the book, tracing immigration from China and connecting that to anti-Asian sentiment in the United States will be crucial. Students could therefore focus specifically on legislation related to China and how it has evolved over the years, exploring for example the Migration Policy Institute's website, which contains key figures that could aid students in visualizing information related to education, population growth, and health coverage (Echeverria-Estrada & Batalova, 2020). The PBS article (Leon, 2020) also discusses this history with particular attention to the model-minority myth, which would also enhance students' understandings. And, they might also benefit from watching the Tedx talk by Canwen Xu, "I Am Not Your Asian Stereotype" in which she talks about common stereotypes she has dealt with and how she has navigated them. Good Morning America's (2021) "How movies and TV shows dehumanize and hypersexualize Asian Americans" provides a brief overview of the representation of Asians in the media and how problematic portrayals persist. Students might then find their own examples of such harmful representations in current media and write a critique of those based on their learning from the two videos.

This focus on anti-Asian attitudes cannot be discussed without attention to the more recent context of the coronavirus that arose in 2020. Former President Trump's labeling of COVID-19 verbally and through Twitter as the "Chinese Virus," corresponded with a rise in hate crimes against Asian peoples in the United States (Reja, 2021). Despite a World Health Organization Executive saying, "Viruses know no borders and they don't care about your ethnicity, the color of your skin or how much money you have in the bank" (Gstalter, 2020, para. 3), blame, nonetheless, continued to fall on Asian groups and they were therefore the target of physical, emotional, and verbal attacks. At the teacher's discretion, students might explore the connection between hate crimes and this blame, sharing stories they find.

During Reading

Mia's family is immediately treated disparagingly by Mr. Yao, the motel owner, who tells them not to complain and threatens, "there are ten thousand other immigrants who would take your job in two seconds" (Yang, 2018, p. 27). Students could discuss: *How does Mr. Yao show how immigrants are taken advantage of in the United States? Why does Mia's family tolerate his mistreatment—to what extent do they really have choices?* Students may not understand how Mr. Yao can be Tawainese and be so mean to Mia's family, expecting that he might understand what it is like to be in a new country. It is thus crucial that teachers focus on the system of oppression that he, too, has internalized (see Chapter 6 on systemic oppression and Chapter 3 on colorism). As they read, students can continue to note how Mr. Yao mistreats Mia and her family. She notes at one point the toll that working at the motel has taken on her parents, "Every day, the two of them cleaned until well past sunset. They had both lost so much weight. They constantly had sweat stains on their shirts and smelled of Clorox" (p. 67). Later Mia sees that her mother's "nails were practically melting off her hands" (p. 114) due to the cleaning products she had to use. Teachers can ask students to research what rights immigrant-laborers have in the United States as well as how these are often exploited by company owners. They might focus specifically on immigration in their geographic areas for this research or take a broader view of the country as a whole.

Stereotypes of Asians are constantly reflected in the book, and students can note how these connect to their before-reading lessons, especially the Tedx video (Xu, n.d.). For example, at one point Jason is surprised to learn that Mia can play piano and that she had a music teacher in China. He says his father told him, "there's nothing in China except piles of dirt and trash," and that, " you guys liked to sit around and spit on the floor" (Yang, 2018, p. 65). His stereotypes clearly come from what his father has socialized him to believe, trying to separate himself from Chinese people. Later in class, Mia's teacher shows an exaggerated picture of Qin Shi Huang, the first emperor of China, in which his "eyes are ridiculously slanted. His eyebrows went all the way up to his forehead" (p. 87). Teachers can remind students of the Good Morning America video and ask them how this image connects to those depicted in media. Further, teachers can ask questions like: *Why do you think these stereotypes exist? Who benefits from hurtful portrayals? Why?*

Later, during a math challenge in class, Mia was placed on a team with the "popular girls" who, to her surprise, "cheered" (p. 140) when they found out, saying "YES! We got the Chinese girl" (p. 140). Teachers can ask students: *How does this stereotype relate to the model minority? How does this moment make Mia feel? How could the teacher have responded?* Students could then brainstorm a list of common stereotypes with which they are familiar or have experienced and discuss how and why they are inaccurate. They might start with less complex stereotypes like: *What are some stereotypes of middle schoolers? What are some stereotypes of the town where we live?* before moving on to some more complex and systemic stereotypes. Gold (2016) encourages educators to "explore the histories of stereotypes" (para. 5) and to "identify the role of power dynamics in stereotypes" (para. 6) and uses a critique of a Taylor Swift music video to accomplish these tasks with students.

Similar to the presence of stereotypes, microaggressions are pervasive in the novel (see Chapter 8 for teaching about microaggressions). When Mia's mother tells a customer who asked her to take her photo to say "Eggplant," which is similar to saying "Cheese," for a photo for English native speakers, the woman corrects her mother, saying, "You know, it's eggplant . . . eggplant . . . if you're going to say it, you should say it right" (Yang, 2018, p.129). The woman reflects the privileging of English in the United States, and teachers could ask students: *How is being a speaker of multiple languages advantageous in society? Why does the woman in this scene say this to Mia's mother?* Even Lupe, Mia's best friend, expresses the notion that all Asian people are the same, assuming Mia and her mother were like Jason and his mom, asking "Aren't you guys always trying to find a good deal?" (p. 160). Teachers can prompt students to note why this statement hurts Mia and to explore how, in fact, not all people of Asian descent are the same. They could have students explore and draw maps of Asian countries, comparing and contrasting the cultures of at least two different groups.

Regarding cultural differences, Mia shares many ways that Americans and Chinese practice disparate customs. At one point she asks: "Why were Americans always asking kids to go out and play? In China, kids almost never played. They had to sit for exams starting at an early age. Except for family get-togethers, every minute after school was packed with homework, drilling, revision, and dictation" (p. 35). The difference in education systems is transparent here, and having students research this aspect further might be enlightening. Mia also shares that "In China, people do not split the bill. It's considered very rude to do so or to not pay for a friend. As a result, people routinely got into fist fights in restaurants as customers pushed and shoved one another for the bill" (p. 164). And finally, she tells readers, "Chinese people believe that if you receive eight dollars, it's good luck" (p. 126). Teachers might ask students to keep a list of the customs Mia shares as they read and/or to choose one and discuss how it is similar to or different from their own cultural practices. Teachers may have to prompt students on this, asking questions such as: *What are some meals that represent your family? What holidays do you celebrate? What is considered good luck to you?*

Mia's family takes in various other immigrants as the story unfolds. They provide food and a free place to stay because these individuals are struggling just as they are. Mia refers to each as "aunt" or "uncle" because, although they are not blood related, it is Chinese custom to refer to family friends in this way. There is Uncle Ming, who is in trouble with loan sharks (p. 49);

Uncle Li, who made hamburgers at his restaurant and threw one away each day to later fish it out of the dumpster and eat each night (p. 70); and Aunt Ling, who worked in a nail salon and said she never got to see the beach in California because she "spent the entire time hunched over, kneeling on the floor" for women who "complained right in front of her, about their Chinese maids and they were probably taking things because 'don't they all steal'" (p. 113); and Uncle Fung who "used to be an accountant back in China and now was working as a waiter over in Riverside" (p. 150) but was fired because of an issue that arose over a language barrier.

Finally, there is Uncle Zhang, a former engineer, whose heart-wrenching story of having his passport taken away by his boss ends positively with Mia writing a letter pretending to be a lawyer to get it back. Students could keep a running log of each of these stories and research immigrant narratives and perspectives. They could select a famous immigrant's biography to read and create a digital presentation on that person and share in small groups (for a list of famous US immigrants with links to biographies, see Hudson County). They might refer to the myimmigrationstory.com website and read some stories or, if so moved, add their own to the site. As some of the stories are graphic in nature, teachers might want to scan the stories first, choosing some from which students can read and respond. Mia asks, "I could not stop thinking about Uncle Li and how he was willing to do anything, go literally anywhere, even into the belly of a dumpster, to get what he wanted. Was that insanity or courage?" (p. 73). Students could discuss Mia's question here, noting how desperate for food Uncle Li was and what else it could be (besides courage or insanity) that prompted him.

It is important, however, for teachers to not just focus on the struggles Mia and her family face but also to facilitate students also seeing the moments of joy and beauty in Mia's narrative. When the washing machine breaks, and she and her parents have to hand-wash all the towels for guests, readers get a glimpse into their family dynamics. She shares: "That afternoon, my parents and I hopped and hopped and hopped, laughing so hard, we soon forgot we were washing towels" (p. 48). The love between her parents is evident, especially when at one point her mother reassures her father that he hasn't failed her, that he's "not even close" (p. 180) to doing so. Her father also tells Mia that despite their trials in the United States, he does not regret coming because he has her, and later her parents tell her that they appreciate the freedom in the United States. Finally, despite not having a lot of money, Mia's mom makes turkey sandwiches for their family and the weeklies and has a Thanksgiving celebration that is filled with love and gratitude. Teachers could ask students to journal on a choice of prompts: *Describe a time that you've been able to find joy in a time of stress or pain,* or *write about a time that you were in a position of either regret or conviction: What made you feel the way you did?*

After Reading

As referenced above, language is a constant issue for characters in the book. Mia's mother wants her to learn English and prioritizes Mia's learning above her first language because she sees the power it will give her daughter. She worries though, that as someone for whom English is not their primary language, Mia will never be as good as her peers, and she even tells Mia, "You're a bicycle, and the other kids are cars" (p. 145). Instead of thinking badly of the mother, teachers could push students to discuss: *Why does Mia's mom say this—what has made her feel this way? How might Mia's mom have internalized the stereotypes and messages we have previously discussed?* Another language struggle occurs when Uncle Fung shares that he was fired for misunderstanding the use of "hey baby" (p. 150). Mia then makes a "Book of American Phrases and Customs" for him that includes advice such as, "When you hear 'get out of here,' do not actually get out of there. It's just something people say when they're surprised" (p. 152). Students could reflect on this list and the issue of language and discuss how these phrases may be confusing to an English learner. As Mia remembers at one point, *"There are no tenses in Chinese!"* (p. 122), and noting the difficulty in English tenses could help students, especially monolingual speakers, discern what it might be like for someone to learn English.

As an activity, students could expand Mia's list to other phrases they use in their own language practices and provide explanations, similar to Mia's. If resources are available, bringing in someone who speaks another language and is willing to teach a short lesson to students can be helpful, too. If someone comes in and starts speaking in another language, students can begin to feel what it is like to not comprehend. In learning some words and phrases in Mandarin, for example, students who are new to the language can experience how difficult it is to create tonal sounds.

In addition to language as related to immigration, health care is a glaring related topic that arises. Mia does not participate in her physical education class and discloses, "I didn't really *hate* sports. We just didn't have any medical insurance, and my parents didn't want me 'taking any chances'" (p. 56). Many students likely take for granted that they have health insurance through their parents or at school, so bringing this to their attention can help them recognize their privilege. Later, in a pivotal scene, Mia's mother is attacked. Yang writes, "Some people came and tried to break into the front office. They were after the cash register" (p. 174). When Mia's mother heard them and went downstairs, they assaulted her, kicking her stomach and causing her to fall to the ground and then kicking her again in the head. They know they need to take her to the hospital but are afraid because they do not have insurance and are undocumented.

Mia takes the money she has saved to enter an essay contest and gives it to her parents, feeling that her mother's health is most important. They are treated poorly at the hospital, with a nurse asking, "How could you have no insurance?" (p. 177) and being told that because they have free boarding, they did not meet the criteria of the "poverty line" (p. 177). The supervisor insists they owe $3,480 (after a discount) until a doctor intervenes and releases them from the bill but maintains the $150 "basic hospital fee" (p. 179). Students can explore information about the "Poverty Guidelines" (ASPE, 2021) that the US Government provides to understand more about Mia's family's situation. They should also develop an understanding of medical insurance. Stanford University has an accessible site that explains how insurance works and defines key related concepts. Students could read this and design skits in which they are seeking medical insurance and ask questions of a provider. Finally, they could explore why it is difficult for immigrants, especially those who are undocumented, to obtain medical insurance and consider the relationship to their jobs in this problem. Teachers can help students draw connections here through visual flow charts using Mia's family as an example. Jobs without a living wage do not allow for insurance, which does not allow for adequate health care.

Similar to these flow charts, teachers can ask students to draw the two roller coasters to which Lupe refers in the text. She explained that, "According to her dad, there were two roller coasters in America—one for rich people and one for poor people. On the rich roller coaster, people have money, so their kids get to go to great schools. Then *they* grow up and make a lot of money, so *their* kids get to go to great schools" (p. 81–82). But poor people, she says, "We're on a different roller coaster. On our roller coaster, our parents don't have money, so we can't go to good schools, and then we can't get good jobs. So then *our* kids can't go to good schools, and they can't get good jobs, and so on and so forth" (p. 82). Lupe here refers to the reproduction of privilege and poverty in society. Through students' drawings, they can add other aspects that contribute to these cycles, such as access to health care mentioned above. Seeing how these issues are affected by structures and not solely by individual motivation and choice is essential.

INTERSECTIONS

Racism against Black people is evident throughout the book and provides an important additional topic to discuss with readers. Mr. Yao explicitly equates "Black" with "bad," and tells Mia, "Any idiot knows—black people are dangerous " (p. 96). When a car is stolen from the motel, the police harass Hank, a weekly who is a Black man. He tells Mia he is "used to it" because such behavior happens "to all black people in this country. In some way or the other" (p. 100). He exemplifies this point when he defends Mia's mom after she was attacked and is charged for assault and spends the night in jail. Teachers can help students draw connections to racism and police brutality (see Chapter 8 on Black Lives Matter) and ask students: *Why did Hank take the plea? How does this experience now have long-term consequences for him? What should have happened instead?*

Intersections between immigrants and bullying are also apparent. Although Jason and Mia have a contentious relationship, he is the victim of bullying just as she is. She overhears a group at school saying to him, "Take that, Chinese dough boy!" and sees "one of them had his hand on Jason's arm and was twisting it while the other boys were holding Jason back" (p. 42). Mia is bullied for her clothes as well, reflected in one scene she describes: "In the bathroom, a couple of sixth-grade girls were gossiping. 'Her pants! Oh my God, have you seen her pants?' . . . It's like she buys her clothes by the pound . . . My *grandmother* dresses better than her!" (p. 135). Students can reflect on how, in these situations, youth are using ethnicity as a reason to bully and then brainstorm how bystanders could intervene to disrupt the situations (see Chapter 3 on bullying).

IDEAS FOR SOCIAL ACTION

Based on these lessons and discussions, action projects could take a number of directions. One could be a campaign to debunk stereotypes, not just of Asian Americans but of any that students feel are prevalent in their schools and communities. They could conduct an anonymous survey to ascertain data from classmates on what those stereotypes might be and then design related actions such as information sessions, or create and post videos to counter them.

As students will learn a great deal in reading about the treatment of immigrants and policy, especially as it is related to health care, authorization, and citizenship, and after seeing how Mia uses the power of writing to advocate for Uncle Zhang and Hank, students might compose letters to legislators addressing one area of inequity related to immigration and suggesting improvements or supports. For example, they might explore the Boston Medical Center's Immigrant and Refugee Health Center (2022) and view the videos of immigrants they have helped provide for in order to call for similar services in their own areas or simply more like this in the country. Noting the difficulties in becoming authorized or citizens in the United States, they could encourage more direct paths and fewer barriers. Furthermore, students could find local institutions that support immigrants and refugees (see Chapter 4 on refugees) and hold a drive to collect donations and supplies to deliver there.

Extending the during reading strategy of reading famous immigrants' biographies and creating presentations, students could share these widely at a community night or on their school's website. They could likewise share their infographics from the before-reading strategies on immigration that target misconceptions and misunderstandings.

Returning to the doctor who refused to charge Mia's family for their $5,800 hospital bill, students could start a campaign in which they encourage others to use their privileges to take up for people. They could design a hashtag such as #BeTheDoctor or #DontStandBy and give examples of what this means through skits, videos, or poster advertisements. For example, if they see someone being bullied, they can step in or tell an adult. If someone drops their books on their way to class, they can stop and help them pick them up. These are small acts, but they can mean a lot, just as they did to Mia's parents. And these sorts of projects help remind students that social action occurs along a spectrum and does not have to be a large protest or sweeping effort. As such, students may be able to see and feel the effects of making change, which is crucial for their continuing to engage in civic life.

Front Desk is not only a novel that portrays the experiences of immigrants vividly and in such a way that is accessible for middle-grade readers, but it is also a quintessential text for engaging students in social action because that is exactly what Mia does in the book. Her personal social action project, securing investors for the hotel and taking it over, can serve as a model and inspiration for students to see that no matter how old they are, they can enact change in their schools, communities, and worlds.

SUPPLEMENTAL RESOURCES

Connected Young Adult Literature

Other Words for Home by Jasmine Warga
The Distance Between Us (Young Readers Edition) by Reyna Grande
Uprising by Margaret Haddix
Audacity by Melanie Crowder
The Downstairs Girl by Stacey Lee
Illegal by Bettina Restrepo

Connected Young Adult Graphic Novels

The Magic Fish by Trung Le Nguyen
Almost American Girl by Robin Ha

New Kid by Jerry Craft
American Born Chinese by Gene Luen Yang

Connected Poetry

"Before Your Arrival" by Ellen Hagan
"My Tongue is Divided into Two" by Quique Avilés
"Things We Carry on the Sea" by Wang Ping

REFERENCES

Bolter, J. Israel, E. & Pierce, S. (2022). Four years of profound change: Immigration policy during the Trump presidency. Migration Policy Institute. https://www.migrationpolicy.org/research/four-years-change-immigration-trump

Boston Medical Center. Immigrant and refugee health center. https://www.bmc.org/immigrant-refugee-health-center

Budiman, A. (2020). Key findings about U.S. immigrants. *Pew Research Center.* https://www.pewresearch.org/fact-tank/2020/08/20/key-findings-about-u-s-immigrants/

Cohn, D. (2015). How U.S. immigration laws and rules have changed through history. *Pew Research Center. https://www.pewresearch.org/fact-tank/2015/09/30/how-u-s-immigration-laws-and-rules-have-changed-through-history/*

Echeverria-Estrada, C. & Batalova, J. (2020). Chinese immigrants in the United States. Migration Policy Institute. https://www.migrationpolicy.org/article/chinese-immigrants-united-states-2018

Gold, J. (2016). Teaching about stereotypes 2.0. *Learning for Justice.* https://www.learningforjustice.org/magazine/teaching-about-stereotypes-20

Gstalter, M. (2020). WHO official warns against calling it 'Chinese virus,' says 'there is no blame in this.' *The Hill.* https://thehill.com/homenews/administration/488479-who-official-warns-against-calling-it-chinese-virus-says-there-is-no/

Good Morning America. (2021). How movies and TV shows dehumanize and hyperexualize Asian Americans. https://www.youtube.com/watch?v=z3jy-lYhR4A

History.com (2021). U.S. immigration before 1965. *A&E Television Networks.* https://www.history.com/topics/immigration/u-s-immigration-before-1965

Hudson County Community College. (n.d.). Biographies of famous U.S. immigrants. https://library.hccc.edu/c.php?g=366161

Lambert, K. (2022). The ultimate guide to teaching source credibility. *Education World. https://www.educationworld.com/ultimate-guide-teaching-source-credibility*

Leon, A. (2020). The long history of racism against Asian Americans in the U.S. *PBS News Hour. https://www.pbs.org/newshour/nation/the-long-history-of-racism-against-asian-americans-in-the-u-s*

Office of the Assistant Secretary for Planning and Evaluation (ASPE). (2021). 2021 poverty guidelines. https://aspe.hhs.gov/topics/poverty-economic-mobility/poverty-guidelines/prior-hhs-poverty-guidelines-federal-register-references/2021-poverty-guidelines

National Geographic. (2022). United States immigration. *Resource Library Collection.* https://education.nationalgeographic.org/resource/resource-library-united-states-immigration

Nazario, S. (2014). *Enrique's journey (The young adult adaptation): The true story of a boy determined to reunite with his mother.* New York, NY: Random House.

Pottinga, N. (2019). My experiences as an immigrant define me & my work. *United Way Blog.* https://www.unitedway.org/blog/my-experiences-as-an-immigrant-define-me-my-work#

Reja, M. (2021). Trump's 'Chinese virus' tweet helped lead ot rise in racist and anti-Asian Twitter content: Study. *ABCNews.* https://abcnews.go.com/Health/trumps chinese-virus-tweet-helped-lead-rise-racist/story?id=76530148

Standford Vaden Health Services. (2022). How U.S. health insurance works. https://vaden.stanford.edu/insurance-referral-office/health-insurance-overview/how-us-health-insurance-works

U.S. Citizenship and Immigration Services. (2022). The naturalization interview and test. https://www.uscis.gov/citizenship/learn-about-citizenship/the-naturalization-interview-and-test

Vlogbrothers. (2017). Understanding Trump's executive order on immigration. https://www.youtube.com/watch?v=sJYTj-VI_L8

Washington State Historical Society. The Chinese exclusion act of 1881. https://www.washingtonhistory.org/education/educators/curriculum/the-chinese-exclusion-act-of-1882/

Xu, C. (n.d.). I am not your Asian stereotype. *TEDx Boise.* https://www.youtube.com/watch?v=_pUtz75lNaw

Yang, K. (2018). *Front desk.* Scholastic Inc.

Conclusion

In the preceding chapters, we have described ten texts for middle-grade readers that each tackles a social justice issue, and we have suggested strategies for teaching about topics as well as ideas for engaging students in related social action. We know that all teachers may not have access to or interest in these specific texts, and thus we hope that these illustrations can serve as examples that might be adapted to other texts with perhaps the same or similar topics. We also encourage teachers to consider how excerpts, short stories, canonical pairings, or choice novels could be used, recognizing the limitations of scripted curriculum and pacing guides many are expected to follow in their districts and states.

In addition, we know that our world is changing daily. Some topics may be foregrounded during certain times and others arise with the times. We hope that teachers can use what we provided to respond to the demands of their contexts and contemporary moments. Geographic location may necessitate, for example, a greater focus on immigration or the refugee crisis. Local protests could encourage an emphasis on Black Lives Matter, or state legislation could warrant attention to sexuality and stigma. Connecting the world to students' education in meaningful ways not only proves its value but also can help them become the participants in our democratic society that we want them to be.

Furthermore, we assert that this sort of learning cultivates students' literacies—in both the traditional sense of reading and writing and from the perspectives of critical and new literacies in terms of having students engage in discourse communities as activists and thinkers. Following Gholdy Muhammad's (2020) model of historically responsive literacy, we believe that "this shouldn't be an either/or challenge" (p. 59) where skills and criticality are in opposition. Rather, we can accomplish them together with thoughtful instruction. And, as Linda Christensen stated, "We don't do social justice . . . at the expense of students' gaining the kind of skills that they need to traverse the world" (Golden, 2008, p. 60). In each chapter, we delineate assignments and activities that include research, writing, reading, and speaking and do so in ways that require students to use those skills toward action.

As mentioned in the Introduction, we use a process for student action that we call *COAR* (Boyd, 2017; Boyd & Darragh, 2019) to scaffold students through the process. While we avow the import of students' selection of topic and problem, as this work *must* cultivate and support youth agency, we have found that implementing a structure and steps (even if messy and not entirely linear) ensures that students can complete the tasks and feel successful. It also provides teachers with tangible materials to evaluate. Teachers can have students submit steps of the process as they work, which can serve as formative assessments to inform teachers of what mini-lessons and additional instruction students may need, or they can have students create and submit final portfolios. The approach is intentionally flexible so that teachers and students can amend it to their learning contexts and needs.

Ultimately, we hope this book serves the many educators and students who desire action to disrupt the systems of oppression rampant in our society. Although not the only place where social change is possible, education is one area where it can be made, and as such, we hope that teachers will embrace the opportunity—and responsibility—to create a better and more just world.

REFERENCES

Boyd, A. (2017). *Social justice literacies in the English classroom: Teaching practice in action.* Teachers College Press.

Boyd, A. & Darragh, J. (2019). Critical literacies on the university campus: Engaging pre-service teachers with social action projects. *English Teaching: Practice & Critique, 19*(1), 49–63.

Golden, J. (2008). A conversation with Linda Christensen on social justice education. *English Journal,* 97(6), 59–64.

Muhammad, G. (2020). *Cultivating genius: An equity framework for culturally and historically responsive literacy.* Scholastic.

Index

accessibility, 84–85
adoption, 58, 59
Adverse Childhood Experiences, 2
ally, 98–99
asylum-seeker, 39
assistive technology, 82

beauty, 80
Benefits of Being an Octopus, 14
Bharatanatyam dance, 79
biracial identity, 97
Black Lives Matter, 89
Blended, 90–91
Boldt Decision, 54
Brando, Marlon, 56
bullying, 8, 17–18, 21, 25–27, 29, 58, 84, 107, 122

caste systems, 81
Chief Seattle, 54
child marriage, 46
Child Welfare Information Gateway, 102
Chinese Exclusion Act of 1882, 113
citizenship test, 116
classroom community, xviii
COAR model, xvii–viii, 128
colorism, 28–29, 32, 117
controversy, xx
courage, teachers,' xxi

cultural differences, 118

Dakota Access Pipeline, 57
deep-breathing techniques, 6, 10
disability, 47, 76–77
Disability Etiquette, 78–79
discussion norms, xviii
divorce, 58, 97
domestic abuse, 20–21, 23, 72

family dynamics, 97
Fish Wars, 54
food insecurity, 44
Fort Lawton, 57
foster care, 21, 58, 101
friendships, 52, 58, 64–65, 82
Front Desk, 114–15

gender roles, 45
Genesis Begins Again, 27
Ghost, 1–2
graphic novel, 43

health care, 19, 83, 120–21
healthy relationships, 73
heteronormativity, 65, 67
homophobia, 64, 70–71

I am Malala, 45

I Can Make this Promise, 52
immigrant rights, 117
immigration, 113–14
Immigration and Nationality Act, 113
implicit bias, 90
Indian Child Welfare Act, 57, 105
Indigenous rights, 51–52
infographics, 73
information (or awareness) campaigns, 34, 48, 73
internalized oppression, 70, 120
International Paralympic Games, 82
intersectionality, 72

King and the Dragonflies, 64–65

land acknowledgements, 59
language, xvii, 34, 42, 65–67, 79, 102, 115, 120
literacies, 127
Littlefeather, Sacheen, 56
Locomotion, 101–2

microaggressions, 55, 84, 92, 94, 118
microresistance, 92
migrant, 39
minimum wage, 15, 22
Missing and Murdered Indigenous Women, 56
model minority, 117

obsessive compulsive disorder, 30
Oppression Olympics, 72

Plateau People's Web Portal, 53
Pew Research Center, 115
picture books, 42, 85
poetry terms, 104
Point Elliot Treaty, 54
police brutality, 90
post-traumatic stress, 94–95
poverty, 8, 15–16, 33, 121; cycle of poverty, 18–19; global poverty, 44, 46.

privilege, 17, 65, 91, 98, 121

questioning (sexuality), 69

racial battle fatigue, 95
racism, 54, 71, 89–90, 106, 122
refugees, 39, 41
refugee camps, 43
resources, 16, 22

self-esteem, 20–21, 31, 35, 105
sexual orientation, 63
sexuality, 65, 67–69
sickle cell anemia, 108–9
small acts of kindness, 83
social action projects, xvii, 8–9, 22–23, 33–34, 47–48, 59–60, 72–73, 84–85, 98–99, 108–9, 122–23
social class, 13–14, 97
Sterling v. Borough of Minersville, et al., 67
stereotypes, 15, 55, 81, 96, 116–17, 122
stigma, 67
substance abuse, 4, 32–33
systemic oppression, 15, 18, 23, 46, 65, 71–72, 77, 91, 117

A Time to Dance, 78
toxic masculinity, 71
trauma, 1, 20, 58–59, 84, 96, 105; and the brain, 3.
tribal sovereignty, 53
Tulalip timeline, 54
Tulalip Reservation, 55

verse, 79, 104

white supremacy, 91
Wolfe, Jayli, 57
women's rights, 44–46
Wounded Knee, 56
When Stars are Scattered, 40
World geography, 42

About the Authors

Ashley S. Boyd is associate professor of English education at Washington State University where she teaches graduate courses on critical theories and anti-oppressive pedagogies and undergraduate courses on Young Adult Literature and Methods for Teaching English. A former secondary English language arts teacher, Ashley's scholarship examines practicing teachers' social justice pedagogies and their critical content knowledges; explores how young adult literature is an avenue for cultivating students' critical literacies; and investigates how students select, organize, and implement social action projects. Her books, including *Social Justice Literacies in the English Classroom: Teaching Practice in Action*, analyze and amplify how teachers subvert traditional classroom curriculum to advance equity and justice. She is co-author, alongside Dr. Janine Darragh, of *Reading for Action: Engaging Youth in Social Justice through Young Adult Literature*, and she has also published in the *Journal of Teacher Education*, *English Education*, and *The ALAN Review*.

Janine Julianna Darragh is associate professor of literacy and English as a new language at the University of Idaho where she teaches courses in Young Adult Literature, teaching students who are culturally and linguistically diverse, and secondary English teacher preparation. A National Board Certified former high school English teacher of thirteen years, with twenty-eight years of teaching experience, her research interests are sociocultural and social justice issues in teaching and learning, young adult literature, and teacher preparation. Her current scholarship focuses on supporting teachers of learners who are culturally and linguistically diverse, teachers of refugees, and teachers in contexts of crisis. She has published in multiple journals such as *English Education, TESOL Journal, English Teaching: Practice &*

Critique, Teaching and Teacher Education, Action in Teacher Education, Curriculum Inquiry, and *The ALAN Review.* This is her second co-authored book with Dr. Ashley Boyd. Their first book *Reading for Action: Engaging Youth in Social Justice through Young Adult Literature* was published in 2019.